THE WORLD, CLOSE TO MIDNIGHT, AND : THE END-TIME:

RAPTURE

THE **MIDNIGHT** - DANIEL'S 70TH WEEK

Jesus said;
"Behold, I come as a thief. Blessed is he
that watcheth, and keepeth his garments,
lest he walk naked, and they see his shame."
Revelation 16:15

Special End-Time Handbook For Every Home: Especially
Christians, worldwide, Pastors, Bishops etc.
Evangelist K. N. Arku-Lawson,
www.pasgom.org

GENEAL COMMENTS, CONTACT ETC

Please, after reading this book, if you have comments, remark,
criticisms, opinion, or anything statement related to this book, send to
any of the following ;

Email addresses;
RaptureMidnight@pasgom.org
RaptureMidnight@gmail.com
RaptureMidnight@yahoo.com

OTHER CONTACTS:

Telephone: + 233 – (0) 540 – 034 - 958
Email: pasgom@gmail.com
Stay blessed
K.N. Arku-Lawson
Evangelist and Revivalist
www.pasgom.org/
www.pasgom.com/

Designed by Qualitype Company Limited
Tel: (233) 302 325266, 325267. **Fax:**(233) 302 325268
Email: siawgeorge@yahoo.com / mrbrownlovesu@yahoo.com

DEDICATION:

This book is dedicated to;

GOD, THE FATHER;
GOD, THE SON;
GOD, THE HOLY GHOST:

I wish to thank the Lord for dropping the idea of writing this book into my Spirit, and also making it possible for its physical manifestation, for the benefit of the world, especially Christians.

Apostle Paul said in 1 Corinthians16:9;
"For a great door and effectual is opened unto me, and there are many adversaries." 1 Corinthians16:9

Soon after commencement of work on this book, it was detected on the 'radar screen' of the kingdom of darkness. Intense efforts were made to hinder it, but to no avail, for the Lord of Host was with me to sustain this noble work, making it a success.

Therefore, all Glory to God, the father, the Son, and the Holy Ghost. Amen. This book, like the anointed stone of David, is being deliberately released, to bring down the Goliaths, who operate against the salvation of multitudes across the nations of the world, and to wake up the ALL THE 'VIRGINS'

God's desire for His Church is that; the 'Virgins' shall be wise, and ask for enough oil, stay awake, for the Midnight is close, the wedding bells are ringing, the Heavenly trumpeter is ready with his MIDNIGHT trumpet, ready for the 'MIDNIGHT' call of God's true Children, who are ready for the air-lift.

Secondly, this book is also dedicated to all true Christians, Pastors and Church leaders that will be bold enough to trumpet this book, and its content, from their respective roof-tops, in various churches. If you are one of such, may God open a special book of remembrance for you and your Ministry, wherever you live in on planet Earth!

Surely, the zeal of the Lord will perform Psalm 3:3 in your life.

"But thou, O LORD, art a shield for me; my glory, and the lifter up of mine head." Psalm 3:3

As you lift the name of the Lord up, May your head, also, be lifted up as you join the great company of those who publish the Good News to the world, as indicated in Psalm 68:11.

This book has been written, but whether your friends and love ones will hear about it, and benefit from it or not, depends on your willingness to publish the news to them.

Remember Psalm 68:11;

"The Lord gave the word: great was the company of those that published it." Psalm 68:11

My prayer for you is that you will join the "...the great company of those that published" God's word, the Good News, for others to hear about this END-TIME EVENT and be ready for the GREAT call;.

"...., Come up hither. And they ascended up to heaven in a cloud; and their enemies beheld them." Revelation 11:12

As you bless others with this book, be blessed also!

CONTENT

ABOUT THE AUTHOR

Chapter 1

INTRODUCTION

A   Controversies over Christian doctrines

It is an undeniable fact that several controversies, or confusions, exist in the Body of Christ, today. These opposing or contrary views, usually, are over cardinal Christian doctrines. Most of these controversies or confusions, as in normal life situations, stem from differences in opinion. However, this time round, it is over differences in interpretations of Scripture – a Spiritual issue.

But should interpretation of scripture, be of private interpretation? Certainly not! If all the parties, involved in the spiritual disputes, claim to have the Holy Ghost, does that mean the Holy Ghost gives different meaning concerning the same issue? Certainly not! For God cannot be the author of confusion!

Perhaps, what we need to do is to re-access the authenticity of our dependence on the Holy Ghost and make amends. This, if done, will better enhance the proper evaluation and understanding of our Church's doctrines, and beliefs, which we often hold so dear without ever daring to question.

Amazingly, concerning each controversy, often, each ministry, church, group or denomination, claims to be on the right path, and that others are wrong. Of course, such differences are not new. It dates back to even the early church.

Remember the case of Paul and Barnabas! They had an incredible sharp disagreement over a rather seemingly harmless issue. On a lighter note, you may choose to call it the "doctrinal differences over John Mark". The whole issue had to do with whether to include or exclude John Mark on a missionary Journey – a journey intended to win souls for Christ. Surprisingly, the disagreement was so sharp that each of them took an entrenched position, pulling them apart, at least, for that trip. This resulted in their departure in separate ways. The same John Mark, who was rejected by Paul, was later considered to be profitable to Paul, a radical shift from an initial entrenched position to a more conciliatory position, perhaps, after a more careful thought, and dependence on God.

Perhaps, this could be a lesson for us to learn from, about the need to revaluate our stand, to be very sure we are heading the right way, especially, over a seemingly sharp difference in doctrinal issues.

In our contemporary times, that type of sharp divergence in opinion, which existed between Paul and Barnabas, could easily constitute a 'good' basis, for some Church leaders, today, even to break away, to establish a new church - a decision, sometimes, totally devoid of complete dependence on God, for His direction.

Focal scripture - Luke 21:35

BEWARE: *The scripture that must be watched closely is;* Luke 21:35.

Jesus said; "For as a <u>snare</u> shall it come on all them that dwell on the face of the whole earth." Luke 21:35.

A The goal, Crucial outcomes, derived, from the above key objectives!
By achieving the stated objectives, above, the following outcomes will

become very obvious, thereby helping us to arrive at crucial conclusion on the issues under discussion.

The link between the main objectives and the corresponding outcomes could be summarized as follows:

The main objectives	The outcomes, if the objective is successfully achieved	Goal to be achieved
Establish the fact that; Christ Second coming has more than one phase; And that it is not just one-time event.	Proves that each of these phases of Christ's second coming, must accomplish a certain specific agenda	To assist the reader to see the vital need to be ready to meet Christ at all times
To determine what each of these phases of Christ second coming is exactly expected to achieve.	Identify the stake or interest of the various categories of Saints of God for each phase.	To assist the reader to be better and properly positioned in Christ
To identify which category of people, on planet earth, will be impacted by each phase, once these momentous events begin to unfold.	This will help to distinguish between the positional levels of Saints, regarding their faithfulness and love relation with Christ	To help the reader to know that spiritual mediocrity can be very costly.

To determine the exact vital milestones of various phases of Christ second coming in relation to the entire End time period.	This will help to identify the root causes of conflicts in opinion or controversies surrounding pre, mid, post tribulation, and to help to pin-point the elements of truth in each of them	To help the reader to be better equipped to help others who may also be confused
To reveal the great dangers false prophets will pose to inhabitants on planet earth in the end time.	This will help Christians, to be more wary, cautious and test the source of every spirit, and try hard to avoid this eternal death traps	To assist the reader to avoid Satanic traps in the end time and avoid God's undiluted wrath
To determine the purpose of the Tribulation and the Great Tribulation	This will further help explain if all category of Saint will go though, tasting the Tribulation or not.	To assist the reader to avoid defilement of his or her garment
To outline the actual horrors of the Great tribulation.	To motivate everybody to avoid this danger.	To assist the reader to be always Heavenly conscious

"Behold, I come as a thief..."
Revelation 16:15

God's word said;

"So shall my word be that goeth forth out of my mouth: it shall not return unto me void, but it shall accomplish that which I please, and it shall prosper in the thing whereto I sent it."
Isaiah 55:11

Possible Rapture questions, on the readers mind

Among the questions this book seeks to address comprehensibly are questions such as;

- Rapture: Is it real or just someone's wishful thinking?
- Rapture, is it in the Bible or not?
- Is Rapture a New Testament doctrine, or dates back to the Old Testament?
- Where, exactly, is Rapture mentioned in the Bible? Just tell me!
- If Rapture is real, then when exactly in relation to great Tribulation will it occur?
- Is the time of the glorious appearance of Jesus Christ predictable, after Rapture?

- Who will be counted worthy to experience Rapture?
- Which of these Rapture doctrines is the right one? Is it pre tribulation, pre-wrath, mid tribulation of post tribulation or which?
- Rapture, if real, will it occur in phases, that is; is it one event, or two, or three etc?
- What happens after Rapture?

Jesus Christ, said;

"So likewise ye, when ye see these things come to pass, know ye that the kingdom of God is nigh at hand." Luke 21:31

Chapter 2

THE SIGNS OF THE END-TIMES

The Bible emphatically declares that the end of the world, that is, the end of human kingdoms, will come someday. Numerous End-time signs are listed in the Bible, as a guide, to forewarn us.

Our Lord, Jesus Christ, specifically, stated that in Mark 13:29
"So ye in like manner, when ye shall see these things come to pass, know that it is nigh, even at the doors." Mark 13:29

"So likewise ye, when ye shall see all these things, know that it is near, even at the doors. Matthew 24:33

What then are the things mentioned that point to the End-time?

A   Signs of the End times – Before and during the Tribulation;
Matthew 24:5-15
Those events are called the Signs of the End times, and are listed as follows scriptures; Matthew 24:3 -15

Highlights
1   "For many shall come in my name," said Jesus Christ
2   Some shall say "I am Christ"; and shall deceive many. ;
3   And ye shall hear of wars and rumors of wars:;
4   For nation shall rise against nation, and kingdom against kingdom
5   And there shall be famines, and pestilences,
6   Earthquakes in divers places.
7   Then shall they deliver you up to be afflicted, and shall kill you;

8 And ye shall be hated of all nations for my name's sake.
9 And then shall many be offended,
10 Many shall betray one another;
11 Many shall hate one another;
12 And many false prophets shall rise; and shall deceive many.
13 And because iniquity shall abound, the love of many shall wax cold;
14 And this gospel of the kingdom shall be preached in all the world;,

B Other Signs of the End times - preceding Tribulation 2 Tim 3:1-7

1 In the last days; perilous times shall come;
2 For men shall be lovers of their own selves,
3 Covetous;
4 Boasters;
5 Proud,
6 Blasphemers,;
7 Disobedient to parents;
8 Unthankful,
9 Unholy;
10 Without natural affection;
11 Trucebreakers;
12 False accusers;
13 Incontinent;
14 Fierce;
15 Despisers of those that are good;
16 Traitors;
17 Heady;
18 High-minded;
19 Lovers of pleasures more than lovers of God;
20 Having a form of godliness, but denying the power thereof:;
21 Lead captive silly women laden with sins, led away with divers lusts;
22 Ever learning, and never able to come to the knowledge of the truth!

C Extra Signs of the End times

1 Signs in the sun, moon, and the stars
2 Many shall run to and fro

3   Knowledge shall be increased
·   "…upon the earth distress of nations, with perplexity; the sea and the waves roaring;" Luke 21:25

·"But thou, O Daniel, shut up the words, and seal the book, even to the time of the end: many shall run to and fro, and knowledge shall be increased." Daniel 12:4

D   The Signs of the Tribulation: the Mid-Night
Apart from the general End-time signs, during the 7- year Tribulation period, there shall be clearer evidence. One of these is the open manifestation of the Anti-Christ. This personality, or figure, will begin as peace-broker, a man of peace, and will be a type of counterfeit of the Prince of Peace. This hint is given in the book of Daniel 8:24 -27.

E   Manifestation of the Anti Christ
This was revealed to Prophet Daniel about 2500 BC, as indicated in Daniel 8:23... "And in the latter time of their kingdom, when the transgressors are come to the full, a king of fierce countenance, and understanding dark sentences, shall stand up."

F   Increased Cataclysmic events and tension
There shall be more terrible Earthquakes, more terrible volcanic eruptions, collision of the Earth with asteroid and meteorites, submergence of vast landmass, wild bushfires consuming vast lands, chaotic occurrences in the sea and rivers, etc
"…, and the stars shall fall from heaven, and the powers of the heavens shall be shaken": Matthew 24:29

G   The signs before the Redemption of Saints
The signs before the redemption of the Saints of God, apply to 2 major events. The signs are in 2 categories.

That is, before;
(1) The Rapture of the Church, and; before;
(2) The Glorious appearance of Christ, to rescue the nation of Israel.

Jesus said in Luke 21:28
"And when these things begin to come to pass, then look up, and lift up your heads; for your redemption draweth nigh".

From this scripture, special signs will precede the redemption of God's people.

But there two types of redemption mentioned in the Bible.
They are;
- The Redemption of the body of Christ - the Church, made up of various categories, or groupings, of Saints – True Christians.
- The Redemption of God's covenant people - the nation of Israel

Hence, the timeline for the redemption depends on which of these two group(s), are under considerations.

Details of these groups, and when they will be delivered, will be discussed later.

"And in the days of these kings the God of heaven will set up a kingdom which shall never be destroyed; and the kingdom shall not be left to other people; it shall break in pieces and consume all these kingdoms, and it shall stand forever." Daniel 2:44

Chapter 3

GOD'S KINGDOM, ANNOUNCED IN DANIEL 2:44-45

A   Brief background

Although several hints are given in the Bible about the coming everlasting Kingdom of God, none is as vivid as the revelations given to Prophet Daniel's, in terms of timelines, and of the preceding vital events.

To recap, due to the SIN of Idolatry, the Jews had been taken into captivity by King Nebuchadnezzar, as prophesied earlier on by prophet Jeremiah around 586 BC.

Whilst in Babylon, the king of Babylon, king Nebuchadnezzar, had a terrible dream, of which he urgently needed interpretation from the wise men of the land. Failure to satisfy the king's difficult request was expected to attract immediate death sentence for all the wise men, including Daniel and his friends.

However, Daniel and his fiends were miraculously promoted by God and shot into prominence, for none of the Babylonian wise men could fulfill the king's demand, except Daniel. Not only did Daniel interpret the dream, but also could make known the dream itself to the King, which the King - the dreamer, had forgotten. In this dream, God's revealed his future plans to bring to an end the kingdom of men, and to establish His own Everlasting Kingdom, a kingdom that never shall come to an end as stated in Daniel 2:44-45:

B   Highlights of Daniel 2:44-45

From Daniel 2:44-45, the following facts were made bare;

- The reign of the kings of the earth will be terminated one day
- God's kingdom will replace human kingdoms
- God's kingdom, once ushered in, will never have an end

From the above revelation, it is no longer a matter of 'if', but 'when' will God's kingdom come, and how will that kingdom come?

The answer to these momentous questions are encapsulated in, what is famously referred to as, Daniels 70 weeks vision,

Angel Gabriel said to Daniel;

"Seventy weeks are determined upon thy people and upon thy holy city, to finish the transgression, and to make an end of sins, and to make reconciliation for iniquity, and to bring in everlasting righteousness, and to seal up the vision and prophecy, and to anoint the most Holy." *Daniel 9:24;*

Chapter 4

THE JEW'S 70 YEARS IN CAPTIVITY AND DANIELS 70 WEEK'S VISION

A Source of information

At the time the Jews were taken to captivity, Daniel and his friends were at a tender age, and many things were unknown to them at the time.

However, over time, Daniel discovered that they were to serve 70 years in captivity, as clearly stated by Jeremiah the Prophet, before the Jews were captured by King Nebuchadnezzar of Babylon.

The source of Daniel's information was from the books, and having obtained this crucial information, he quickly took the next step, to petition the God of Heaven concerning Jerusalem and the entire state of affairs of that nation, which was in captivity.
This is found in Daniel 9:1 -2

B Highlight of Daniel 9:1-2

The highlights from Daniel 9:1-2, are;
1. Daniel understood by the books after a carefully research.
2. Information about their captivity had been foretold by Prophet Jeremiah
3. That the desolation of Jerusalem was to last 70 years.
4. That they, the Jews, were to serve for only 70 years in captivity, and no more.

With above awareness, Prophet Daniel moved to the next stage of seeking God's face through prayer, thereby petitioning Heaven, as stated earlier on. This move of Prophet Daniel, as an intercessor, served as trigger for many other VITAL revelations, soon to be pointed out. God found a man He could trust with information about His future plans for Israel and also for the whole world. And these unfolding revelations hold the key to the destiny of entire world. To repeat, this vision includes, or encircles, the Nation of Israel, that is, the Jews; the Holy people, that is, the 'followers of the messiah', which is the church, as well as the fate of the rest of all other people outside the Church, etc.

C Events leading to Daniels 70 week's vision

As indicated earlier, based on information obtained by Daniel, he saw the urgent need to approach God, seek his face regarding the rebuilding of the ruined city of Jerusalem.

The book of remembrance for Jerusalem was immediately opened, through Daniels earnest petition to the throne of grace.

D The trigger for Daniels 70 week's vision

The trigger for what is now known as Daniels 70 week's vision was the faith in God, exhibited in prayer by one man, Prophet Daniel. This is captured in Daniel 9:3 -19;

E Highlight of Daniel's prayer Daniel 9:3-19

- Daniel sought the face of the Lord concerning their plight in captivity.
- He recounted events leading to their shame, disgrace, affliction, and the desolation of Jerusalem
- He confessed the Sins of his forefathers
- He acknowledged that that he was not making the petition based on their righteousness, but by God's grace.
- He asked for mercy
- He petitioned the God of Heaven, to remove the curse.
- He made supplication for restoration of their dignity, for God's name sake.
- He asked God not to delay in granting the request

F The response to Daniel's prayer

With this sincere supplication, came God's response through Angel

Gabriel's visitation to Daniel, as indicated in Daniel 9:20 -22

G   Highlights of Daniel 9:20-22
- The answer to his prayer was instantaneous
- He got more than his request in his prayer.
- He was given skill and understanding, to understand events yet to take place
- This encounter ushered in, perhaps, the most important revelation ever for the end time.
- This revelation is well known as Daniels 70 week's vision

H   Daniel's 70 week's vision -The blueprint for the entire End time of the world!

Not only was the request in the prayer of Daniel answered, but also the stage was set for extra Revelation. Conveyed to Daniel, was God's blue print for the Nation of Israel; as well as of all the Holy people of God. All this is encapsulated in what is called 'Daniel's 70 week vision'. This, certainly, marks the summary of the beginning of the GREATEST revelation concerning both;
- The Nation of Israel and
- The Church of Jesus Christ.

A clear understanding of this vision, and its fallouts, is crucial in placing the entire End Time events in their proper perspective. This, certainly, is the blueprint of both the plan of Salvation of the world, and all other End-Time events.

In fact, this revelation holds the key to exact identity of the Messiah, in terms of the time of His Manifestation, His death, and the vital events that will, finally, culminate into the establishment of His Kingdom.

Also other issues; like the manifestation of the Antichrist in terms of the time of his manifestation; how long he will rule; his covenant with Israel; the breaking of this covenant, his demand for worship etc are all coded in this vision.

As indicated at the earlier part of this book, some prophesies are coded, and therefore needs to be decoded for clearer understanding.

The vision, from God, was delivered through His messenger, Angel Gabriel, to Daniel. The full text is found Daniel 9:24 -27;

I   Highlights of the 70 week's vision are;
- Seventy weeks are determined upon thy people and upon thy holy city;
- To Finish the transgression, and to make an end of sins, and to make reconciliation for iniquity,
- To bring in everlasting righteousness, and to seal up the vision and prophecy;
- To anoint the Most Holy.
- There shall be seven weeks, and threescore and two weeks, that is 69 weeks.
- The street shall be built again, and the wall, even in troublous times.
- Messiah be cut off, but not for himself:
- The people of the prince that shall come shall destroy the city and the sanctuary; and the end thereof shall be with a flood, that is troubles.
- And he shall confirm the covenant with many for one week; that is referring to a peace treaty.
- And in the midst of the week he shall cause the sacrifice and the oblation to cease; that is the breaking of the peace treaty.
- The overspreading of abominations, he shall make it desolate, even until the consummation, and that determined shall be poured upon the desolate."

J   Further breakdown of the 70 week's vision
- A period, or time span, of 70 week, based on divine calculations, had been imposed by God on the nation of Israel to finish paying for their sins.
- The prophetic clock was to start from a certain specific time.
- The starting time was time the command was issued to start the

rebuild the walls of Jerusalem and the streets, which was previously destroyed and set on fire.

- There shall be 7 Specific accomplishments by the end of the 70 weeks
- The 70 weeks is to be divided into two parts, part 1 and part 2
- The part 1 was to last for 69 weeks, ending with death of the messiah
- The part 2, beginning at a later date, and will last for 1 week
- The total, in effect is 70 weeks, by angelic calculations.
- The part 2 begins with an agreement between Israel and false messiah, a supposed Peace-maker – the Anti Christ.
- The false peacemaker, the Anti Christ, will betray Israel, terminating the agreement in the middle of the 1 week.
- The false peacemaker – the Anti Christ will further project himself as a type of God, demanding worship, an abominable request
- This will trigger the wrath of the almighty God upon the Anti-Christ.
- The end of part 2 of time frame, also corresponds with the end of sins
- Unlike the end of part 1, where the messiah died, the end of part 2, ushers in the Everlasting Kingdom of the messiah.
- The part 2 time frame will be a time of extreme pain for Israel and all who dwell in the entire world.

K   The 7 Specific outcomes within the Daniels 70 weeks

It is very important to note that by the end of the 70 weeks, there ought to be 7 specific accomplishments, to be sure the 70 weeks have truly ended.

This is crucial, and is captured in Daniel 9:24
"…to finish the transgression, and to make an end of sins, and to make reconciliation for iniquity, and to bring in everlasting righteousness, and to seal up the vision and prophecy, and to anoint the most Holy…"

From Daniel 9:24, by the end of the entire Daniel's 70 weeks, the time Christ starts His reign on earth, the following 7 specific things are expected to have been achieved. They are;

1. Finish transgression
2. Make an end of sins
3. Reconciliation for iniquity
4. Bring in everlasting righteousness
5. To seal up the vision
6. And prophesy
7. To anoint the Most Holy

Chapter 5

ANALYSIS OF DANIELS 70 WEEKS' VISION

The vision has two parts. They are;

A Part 1: The 69 weeks period. Daniel 9:25, 26.
" Know therefore and understand, that from the going forth of the commandment to restore and to build Jerusalem unto the Messiah the Prince shall be seven weeks, and threescore and two weeks: the street shall be built again, and the wall, even in troublous times.

9:26 And after threescore and two weeks shall Messiah be cut off, but not for himself: and the people of the prince that shall come shall destroy the city and the sanctuary; and the end thereof shall be with a flood, and unto the end of the war desolations are determined." Daniel 9:25, 26.

From the above scripture, the ticking of the prophetic clock began; "...from the going forth of the commandment to restore and to build Jerusalem..."

The entire prophetic calendar, or timetable, is expected to span over a total period of 70 weeks. However, it is important to stress that there are coded meanings in this vision. The coded meanings may be referred to as some of the mysteries of the kingdom of God. This similar to what our Lord and Savior Jesus Christ said to the disciples;
"... It is given unto you to know the mysteries of the kingdom of heaven, but to them it is not given." Matthew 13:11

Note: It is important to know that Daniel's 1 week is the equivalence of 7 years in the world of humans.

Going by the earthly calendar, therefore, 70 weeks will last for, or span over, a total period 70 x 7 years = 490 years, beginning from a specified date, stated in the prophesy.;

However, these 490 years was also to be split into two parts. These two parts are:
Part 1: This is from the time the command to rebuild Jerusalem was given, to the time the Messiah was cut – off, that is, killed. This is found in Daniel 9:25-26, was to last a total of 69 weeks = 69 x 7 = 483 years

B Part 2 - Daniels 70th week: - The midnight period

This is also called Daniels 70th week. It begins from a certain future date, unknown by humans, but known only by the almighty God alone. This is called the time of the Prince and, that is, from the time the Antichrist manifests openly, to the time his cup become full, that is, the end of reign of the Antichrist. That period, corresponds to the period of the tribulation on Earth - The midnight period.

Furthermore, the Part 2 will also have two parts, that is two 3½ years. The two halves, will total 7year, 2 x 3½ years =7 years

To recap, the entire time frame, as given to Daniel, is 70 weeks. The end of the seventy weeks is to end with the following;
"…..to finish the transgression, and to make an end of sins, and to make reconciliation for iniquity, and to bring in everlasting righteousness, and to seal up the vision and prophecy, and to anoint the most Holy" Daniel 9:23

Certainly, the END of the events, as mentioned in Daniel 9:23 could correspond with no other time in human history other than the END TIME period, that is, just before The Messiah's Kingdom is ushered in as found in Matthew 24: 29-35

I The Midnight and Anti Christ on Earth;
From Daniel 9:27 it is written; "And he shall confirm the covenant with many for one week: and in the midst of the week he shall cause the sacrifice and the oblation to cease, and for the overspreading of abominations he

shall make it desolate, even until the consummation, and that determined shall be poured upon the desolate." Daniel 9:27

In the above scripture, the remaining one week is mentioned in the Daniel's vision is the 70th week. This is called Daniels's 70th week, which corresponds with the last seven years within which the Anti Christ enters into covenant with Israel, only to beak agreement, halfway through the period!

At this time, he the Anti-Christ shall demand worship, first having portrayed himself as god that must be worshipped - the abomination that makes desolate, as mentioned in Daniel 9:27.

This may be called the "MIDNIGHT" periods on the planet Earth, a period of the works of darkness, with untold pain. Simply put, it will be TERRIBLE! Extremely terrible!

For those still dwelling on the Earth by then, especially the Nation of Israel and the remaining Children of God, who may wish to remain loyal God, or stand for God, it is imminent death.

For others, it is preparation for Hell fire.
Hence, prophet Jeremiah said: "Alas! for that day is great, so that none is like it: it is even the time of Jacob's trouble; but he shall be saved out of it" Jeremiah 30:7

Also Revelation 12:12, says;
"Therefore rejoice, ye heavens, and ye that dwell in them. Woe to the inhabiters of the earth and of the sea! for the devil is come down unto you, having great wrath, because he knoweth that he hath but a short time." Revelation 12:12

Also Revelation 8:13, says;
"And I beheld, and heard an angel flying through the midst of heaven, saying with a loud voice, Woe, woe, woe, to the inhabiters of the earth by reason of the other voices of the trumpet of the three angels, which are yet to sound!" Revelation 8:13

C   Part 3
The GAP in the prophetic calendar – The time of GRACE!

The period between the end of the 69 week and the beginning of the 70th week is called the 'GAP in the prophetic calendar'.

Within this period, the Daniel's 70 weeks prophesy is mute. This period is the Church age, that is, almost 2000 years.

i   The Church Age – The GAP in the prophetic calendar.
The Church Age began on the Day of Pentecost, shortly after the Messiah was cut-off, as recorded in Acts chapter 2. It was the time the Holy Ghost, the promise of the Father was 'officially' commissioned, to give birth to the Church.

The Church Age is therefore nearly 2000 years in duration. Within these almost 2000 years, what has God been doing in the meantime? And that brings us to what God has been doing and still doing. This is the Divine work in the prophetic GAP

ii   God's work in the prophetic GAP
During this 2000 year gap, God has been very busy. Through His 'Chief Executive', God the Holy Ghost on the Earth, He is doing a number of things. Among these are;

	God's work	Scriptural References
1	Building His Church.	Praising God, and having favour with all the people. And the Lord added to the church daily such as should be saved. Acts 2:47
		6 i have planted, apollos watered; but god gave the increase. 3:7 so then neither is he that planteth any thing, neither he that watereth; but god that giveth the increase. 3:8 now he that planteth and he that watereth are one: and every man shall receive his own reward according to his own labour. 3:9 for we are labourers together with god: ye are god's husbandry, ye are god's building. i cor. 3;6-9
		12:18 But now hath God set the members every one of them in the body, as it hath pleased him. I Cor 12:18
		21 In whom all the building fitly framed together groweth unto an holy temple in the Lord: 2:22 In whom ye also are builded together for an habitation of God through the Spirit. Eph:21-22

2	Taking out of the nations a people for His Name	
3	Bringing in the fullness of the Gentiles	" … And the Lord added to the church daily such as should be saved. Acts 2:47 For I would not, brethren, that ye should be ignorant of this mystery, lest ye should be wise in your own conceits; that blindness in part is happened to Israel, until the fulness of the Gentiles be come in. Romans 11:25
4	Placing believers into a living organism	12:13 For by one Spirit are we all baptized into one body, whether we be Jews or Gentiles, whether we be bond or free; and have been all made to drink into one Spirit.
5	Saving a "showcase" that will eternally display His matchless grace	2:7 That in the ages to come he might shew the exceeding riches of his grace in his kindness toward us through Christ Jesus. Eph. 2:7
6	Manifesting Himself through His Body which is upon the earth	3:16 And without controversy great is the mystery of godliness: God was manifest in the flesh,

		justified in the Spirit, seen of angels, preached unto the Gentiles, believed on in the world, received up into glory. 1 Tim 3:16

iii The Almighty God, the God of suddenly

Our God is a God of suddenly. The Messiah was suddenly born when the Jews were still 'sleeping', unaware of what was going on. In fact, it was the wise men from the East, and the shepherd, who came to wake them up, and informed them about the unfolding extraordinary events happening in their own land.

It is also important to know note that after the Messiah was cut-off, the Church was also born suddenly, unannounced, whilst they were meeting in the upper room.

"And suddenly there came a sound from heaven as of a rushing mighty wind, and it filled all the house where they were sitting." Acts 2:2

Similarly, just as the Church had a sudden beginning shortly after the conclusion of the 69th week, initiated by the coming of the Holy Spirit on the day of Pentecost, so we should expect the Church to have a sudden removal shortly before the beginning of the 70th week, and that is the RAPTURE of the Church.

D. Daniels prophetic Calendar – summary

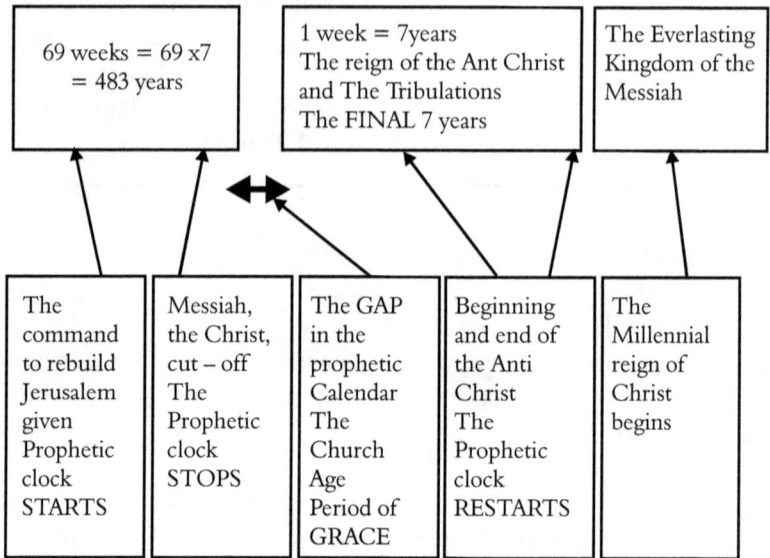

69 weeks = 69 x7 = 483 years	1 week = 7years The reign of the Ant Christ and The Tribulations The FINAL 7 years	The Everlasting Kingdom of the Messiah

The command to rebuild Jerusalem given Prophetic clock STARTS	Messiah, the Christ, cut – off The Prophetic clock STOPS	The GAP in the prophetic Calendar The Church Age Period of GRACE	Beginning and end of the Anti Christ The Prophetic clock RESTARTS	The Millennial reign of Christ begins

E. The Crucial milestones within the Daniels 70 Weeks

From the previous discussion, it is has been made very clear that: the prophetic calendar started ticking from the time the command was given to start re-building of the temple in Jerusalem, and that must be between 458 - 445 BC

| Beginning of the prophetic clock The rebuilding of the Jerusalem and street | 69 weeks 483 years | | 1 week 7 years | Everlasting Righteousness Ushered in by Christ |

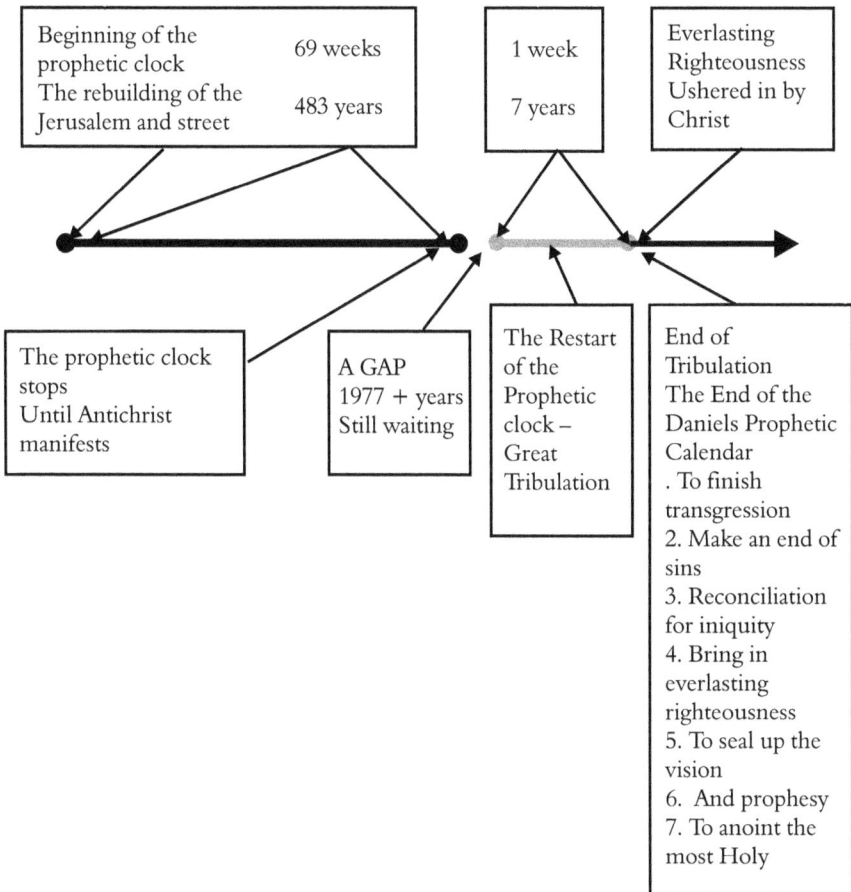

| The prophetic clock stops Until Antichrist manifests | A GAP 1977 + years Still waiting | The Restart of the Prophetic clock – Great Tribulation | End of Tribulation The End of the Daniels Prophetic Calendar . To finish transgression 2. Make an end of sins 3. Reconciliation for iniquity 4. Bring in everlasting righteousness 5. To seal up the vision 6. And prophesy 7. To anoint the most Holy |

Chapter 6

DANIEL'S VISION BY THE RIVER HIDDEKEL;

> *The following vision, given to Prophet Daniel, has lot of crucial information. Buried in it is very crucial information for the children of God. In terms of specificity in end-time timelines, this vision is certainly the most vivid.*

A   Daniels encounter with 'strange men' – the angel

"And in the four and twentieth day of the first month, as I was by the side of the great river, which is Hiddekel; 10:5 Then I lifted up mine eyes, and looked, and behold a certain man clothed in linen, whose loins were girded with fine gold of Uphaz: 10:6 His body also was like the beryl, and his face as the appearance of lightning, and his eyes as lamps of fire, and his arms and his feet like in colour to polished brass, and the voice of his words like the voice of a multitude. 10:7 And I Daniel alone saw the vision: for the men that were with me saw not the vision; but a great quaking fell upon them, so that they fled to hide themselves. 10:8 Therefore I was left alone, and saw this great vision, and there remained no strength in me: for my comeliness was turned in me into corruption, and I retained no strength. 10:9 Yet heard I the voice of his words: and when I heard the voice of his words, then was I in a deep sleep on my face, and my face toward the ground. ….."

B   The promise of sudden deliverance of God people

After several revelations, by the Angel to Daniel, the angel concluded with the following VITAL message, as captures in Daniel 12: 1-12.

C   Crucial Questions and answers by the river Hiddekel;

The encounter between Daniel and the strange men by the river Hiddekel, reveals very important information regarding God's timeline of deliverance, both for the Nation of Israel and the Church in the End time. It is very important to carefully note the context in which the questions were asked and how the answers were given.

First of all, it is vital to trace the root cause of the ensuing questions. After the Angel delivered the long message, it ended with vital a information, thus; 12:1 "…: and at that time thy people shall be delivered, every one that shall be found written in the book"

The question, and answers sessions below, therefore, should be read bearing that in mind.

Key Question 1 – asked by one of the men by the river;
"And one said to the man clothed in linen, which was upon the waters of the river, How long shall it be to the end of these wonders?" Daniel 12:6

VITAL Answer 1 to Question 1
"…it shall be for a time, times, and an half; and when he shall have accomplished to scatter the power of the holy people, all these things shall be finished."

Key Question 2 – asked by Daniel by the river;
"And I heard, but I understood not: then said I, O my Lord, what shall be the end of these things?" Daniel 12:8

VITAL Answer 2 to Question 2
"……And from the time that the daily sacrifice shall be taken away, and the abomination that maketh desolate set up, there shall be a thousand two hundred and ninety days. 12:12 Blessed is he that waiteth, and cometh to the thousand three hundred and five and thirty days." Daniel 12:9-11

D   Analysis of Daniel's vision by the river Hiddekel;
From the questions and answers sessions that took place by the river Hiddekel, as well as vital information captured from the 70th week vision, without any doubt, the following preliminary conclusions are crystal

clear. These deductions are made without any shadow of doubt;
God will deliver His people from the wrath of the Anti-Christ. True or false?

- Only those whose names are in the book shall be delivered. True or false?
- The deliverance will be in phases, having a beginning and ending period. True or false?
- The deliverance for some Saints, will start long before the Anti Christ strikes True or false?
- The deliverance operation would be finished or completed just when he Anti Christ is ready to strike, or scatter, God's people. True or false?
- The entire deliverance process would have been finished just when the Anti Christ has accomplished his preparatory work to scatter God's people. In effect, the deliverance is a process and not just one time event. True or false?
- The first half of the Tribulation, that is 1290 days, will be characterized, comparatively, by a seemingly peaceful posture of the Anti Christ, accompanied by an ongoing terrible cataclysmic event.
- The 'true color' of the Anti Christ will be known mid way through the Tribulation, and that is, the second half of the Tribulation, also lasting 1290 days = 3 ½ years. True or false?
- The second half of the Tribulation, that is, the last 1290 days, will be characterized mainly by a fierce and monstrous posture of the Anti Christ, accompanied by very terrible cataclysmic events, all occurring at the same time. True or false?
- The number 1335, mentioned in Daniel 12:12 is not figurative, but a real, and very important, time interval between two major, and specific, events. Hence, qualified by; "…Blessed is he…."
- The total time interval between the first major event and the last deliverance will be 1335 days = 45 + 1290 days. True or false?
- This implies, the first deliverance operation may occur, at least, 45 clear days before the start of the first half of the Tribulation. That is, pre-tribulation, as will be explained shortly.
- The last deliverance will occur approximately 1335 after the first major event had occurred, and before the beginning of the wrath of the Anti Christ, that is, mid-tribulation, as indicated in this; "……and when he

shall have accomplished to scatter the power of the holy people, all these things shall be finished."

"Blessed is he that waiteth, and cometh to the thousand three hundred and five and thirty days." Daniel 12:12

Chapter 7

THE RAPTURE

A. Meaning of Rapture

To throw more light on the doctrine 'Rapture', its origin may be necessary. The word Rapture is from the Latin word 'Raptus', meaning the state, or experience, of being carried away. Additionally, the Greek word, aJrpavzw, that is, Harpazo, means;

- hold-up;
- Catch (away, up);
- Pluck;
- Pull (by force);
- Take (by force).

This doctrine is found in I Thessalonians 4:17

"…Then we who are alive and remain shall be caught up together" I Thessalonians. 4:17

Some Christians contend that because the word 'Rapture' is not directly found in the Bible, it is not Biblical. Of course, the word 'Rapture' is not directly mentioned in the Bible just as the word Bible is not directly mentioned in the 'Bible'. Yet, with the mentioning of the word 'Bible', no one has problem whatsoever knowing what one is talking about. In fact, the word 'Bible' is unmistakably understood, even by a child, to mean God's word.

In essence, when discussing the authenticity of the Rapture, the focus ought not to be on the word 'Rapture' – as to whether the word exists in the Bible or not, but rather on what Rapture means or represents in God's word. What does the word Rapture represents in the Bible? That ought to be the core issue. Does what it stands for exist in the Bible. This ought to be the crucial question.

B   Examples of Rapture in the Bible

Are there any prototypes or examples of Rapture in the Bible?
The answer is emphatic 'YES'.

In throwing more light on the answer, examples of Old and New Testament bodily ascension to Heaven are given, as well as the listing of the corresponding scriptures, each followed by a corresponding question, as a food for thought. .
Remember, God asked a very important question in Jeremiah 32:27,
"Behold, I am the LORD, the God of all flesh: is there any thing too hard for me?" Jeremiah 32:27. The answer is obvious.

The examples below are just a foretaste of much greater things to come. In fact they are the models of the actual building.

C   Examples of Saints, 'caught up' or who experience Rapture

	Scripture reference	Food for thought
Enoch	And Enoch walked with God: and he was not; for God took him, Genesis 5:24. This means Enoch was caught up to Heaven by God and did not die physically here on Earth. This is classic example Rapture of the living	• Did Enoch die before going to Heaven? • "For God took him," to where?
Elijah	And it came to pass, as they still went on, and talked, that, behold, [there appeared] a chariot of fire, and horses of fire, and parted them both asunder; and Elijah went up by a whirlwind into heaven. 2 Kings 2:11 This also means Elijah was caught up to Heaven by God and did not die physically here on Earth. This is another classic example of Rapture of the living	• Did Elijah die before going to Heaven? • If Elijah went up without dying, is it too hard for God to replicate the same? • Could this depict the Rapture of the living?

Jesus Christ	And it came to pass, while he blessed them, he was parted from them, and carried up into heaven. Luke 24: 51 This also means Jesus Christ was caught up to Heaven by God after he died and resurrected physically here on Earth. This is a classic example of Rapture of the resurrected dead.	• Did Jesus Resurrect? • Could this depict the Rapture of the resurrected dead?
Philip	"And when they were come up out of the water, the Spirit of the Lord caught away Philip, that the eunuch saw him no more: and he went on his way rejoicing." Acts 8:39 This also means Philip was caught away from the Ethiopian eunuch and saw him no more. This is a classic example of Rapture out of sight, never to be seen again by friends still on Earth	• Could this be a model of how Saints will disappear from the world?
The two Jewish Tribul ation Proph ets	And they heard a great voice from heaven saying unto them, Come up hither. And they ascended up to heaven in a cloud; and their enemies beheld them. Revelation 11:12 This also means the two Jewish Tribulation Prophets were caught away from the Earth and seen no more. This is a classic example of Rapture out of sight, with a loud shout, never to be seen again by friends still on Earth	• "Come up hither". Could this be a Rapture call? • "They ascended up to heaven". Could this be an example of Rapture of the resurrected dead, and also example of Rapture of the Tribulation Saints?

D Is Rapture too difficult for God?

Having seen the above practical cases, this question is personally for you. Can God change multitude of people in a split second, and transport them out of the world to a secret location outside the Earth?

Hint: As you attempt to answer this question, it is important to remember that the earth itself hangs on nothing. If it is sustained by God's power, what is it that He cannot do?

In Job 26:7, God's word declares;
"..He stretcheth out the north over the empty place, and hangeth the earth upon nothing." Job 26:7

God's is personally asking you
"Behold, I am the LORD, the God of all flesh: is there any thing too hard for me?" Jeremiah 32:27
Answer: Absolutely nothing! Hope this is your answer, too.

E. Direct scriptural references, pointing to Rapture

Scriptural references	Scriptures	Food for thought
Daniel 12:1	… and there shall be a time of trouble, such as never was since there was a nation even to that same time: and <u>at that time thy people shall be delivered,</u> every one that shall be found written in the book.	• Who are the people mentioned here? • How will the people be delivered? • When exactly will this occur?
Matthew 24:40	"And while they went to buy, the bridegroom came, and <u>those who were ready went in with him to the wedding; and the door was shut.</u> 11"Afterward the other virgins came also, saying, 'Lord, Lord, open to us!' 12"But he answered and said, 'Assuredly, I say to you, I do not know you.' 13"<u>Watch therefore, for you know neither the day nor the hour in which the Son of Man is coming.</u>	• Will there be a marriage for the lamb • Who is the Bridegroom here? • Those who were ready went with the Bridegroom. How did they go? • Who will be the Bride at this wedding? • When will the wedding of the lamb take place? • Where will wedding take place?

I Corinthians 15:50-52	50 Now this I say, brethren, that flesh and blood cannot inherit the kingdom of God; nor does corruption inherit incorruption. 51 Behold, I tell you a mystery: <u>We shall not all sleep, but we shall all be changed 52 in a moment, in the twinkling of an eye, at the last trumpet. For the trumpet will sound, and the dead will be raised incorruptible, and we shall be changed.</u>	• "The dead will be raised incorruptible." Raised from the dead to where? • When will this happen? • ...and we shall be changed. Into what body? • Changed to stay on earth or transported elsewhere?
Revelation 3:10	...Because thou hast kept the word of my patience, <u>I also will keep thee from the hour of temptation, which shall come upon all the world,</u> to try them that dwell upon the earth.	• Who are they, the keepers of word of His Patience? • How will the Saints be kept from the hour of temptation? • Hidden on earth or taken away?
Daniel 12:12	<u>Blessed is he that waiteth, and cometh to the thousand three hundred and five and thirty days</u>	• That waitheth for what? • From what time to what time? • "and cometh" to where? • Which group of saints will be expected to wait? • Note : The 1335 days mentioned in Daniel 12:12 very, very, very well

*THE WORLD, CLOSE TO MIDNIGHT, AND : THE END-TIME: **RAPTURE***

Mark	13:35 Watch ye therefore: for ye know not when the master of the house cometh, at even, or at midnight, or at the cockcrowing, or in the morning:	• Will this type of coming be announced or sudden?
Mark	13:32 But of that day and that hour knoweth no man, no, not the angels which are in heaven, neither the Son, but the Father. 13:33 Take ye heed, watch and pray: for ye know not when the time is. 13:34 For the Son of man is as a man taking a far journey, who left his house, and gave authority to his servants, and to every man his work, and commanded the porter to watch. 13:35 Watch ye therefore: for ye know not when the master of the house cometh, at even, or at midnight, or at the cockcrowing, or in the morning: 13:36 Lest coming suddenly he find you sleeping. 13:37 And what I say unto you I say unto all, Watch.	• Will this type of coming be announced or sudden?
Luke	17:26 And as it was in the days of Noe, so shall it be also in the days of the Son of man. 17:27 They did eat, they drank, they married wives, they were given in marriage, until the day that Noe entered into the ark, and	• Will this type of coming be announced or sudden?

The location of the Bride and saints, before God's wrath was poured on the earth, clearly points to Rapture. *Please, look at this very carefully*

INDIRECT REFERENCES TO RAPTURE	VERY IMPORTANT
And I saw another sign in heaven, great and marvellous, seven angels having the seven last plagues; for in them is filled up the wrath of God. 15:2 And I saw as it were a sea of glass mingled with fire: <u>and them that had gotten the victory over the beast, and over his image, and over his mark, and over the number of his name, stand on the sea of glass, having the harps of God.</u> Revelation 15:1-2	• Which group of Saints are these? • Did this Saints experience the 7 last plaques during the Tribulation? • <u>stand on the sea of glass,?</u> • <u>Where is that sea of glass located?</u> • On earth or outside the earth? • If outside the earth, then when were the Saints up picked from the Earth? •What name must be given to the process of picked Saints from the Earth?
"And there came unto me one of the seven angels which had the seven vials full of the seven last plagues, and talked with me, saying, Come hither, I will shew thee the bride, the Lamb's wife. 21:10 And he carried me away in the spirit to a great and high mountain, and shewed me that great city, the holy Jerusalem, descending out of heaven from God, Revelation 21:9	• Come hither, I will shew thee the bride, the Lamb's wife? • Was this before or after the seven last plagues were poured?

F Indirect references, strongly pointing to Rapture
In this section you will find;
• Where Bride was before the seven last plagues during the Tribulation were poured

- The Angel, as it were, assures St. John that God is concerned about the safety of the Bride, and has taken steps to protect the Bride before the seven last plaques are released

The location of the Bride and saints, before God's wrath was poured on the earth, clearly points to Rapture. *Please, look at this very carefully*

INDIRECT REFERENCES TO RAPTURE	VERY IMPORTANT
And I saw another sign in heaven, great and marvellous, seven angels having the seven last plagues; for in them is filled up the wrath of God. 15:2 And I saw as it were a sea of glass mingled with fire: and them that had gotten the victory over the beast, and over his image, and over his mark, and over the number of his name, stand on the sea of glass, having the harps of God. Revelation 15:1-2	• Which group of Saints are these? • Did this Saints experience the 7 last plaques during the Tribulation? • stand on the sea of glass,? • Where is that sea of glass located? • On earth or outside the earth? • If outside the earth, then when were the Saints up picked from the Earth? •What name must be given to the process of picked Saints from the Earth?
"And there came unto me one of the seven angels which had the seven vials full of the seven last plagues, and talked with me, saying, Come hither, I will shew thee the bride, the Lamb's wife. 21:10 And he carried me away in the spirit to a great and high mountain, and shewed me that great city, the holy Jerusalem, descending out of heaven from God, Revelation 21:9	• Come hither, I will shew thee the bride, the Lamb's wife? • Was this before or after the seven last plagues were poured?

G   Direct scriptural references, pointing to glorious appearance of Christ

Scriptural references	Scriptures	Food for thought
Daniel 12:12	11 And from the time that the daily sacrifice shall be taken away, and the abomination that maketh desolate set up, there shall be a thousand two hundred and ninety days.	• When will the abomination that maketh desolate be set up • There shall be 1290 days from when to when?
Revelation 1:7	Behold, he cometh with clouds; and every eye shall see him, and they also which pierced him: and all kindreds of the earth shall wail because of him. Even so, Amen.	• Will these coming be sudden or gradual and progressive? • How does this compare with coming "..as a thief.."
Matthew 24:: 29	Immediately after the tribulation of those days shall the sun be darkened, and the moon shall not give her light, and the stars shall fall from heaven, and the powers of the heavens shall be shaken: 30 And then shall appear the sign of the Son of man in heaven: and then shall all the tribes of the earth mourn, and they shall see the Son of man coming in the clouds of heaven with power and great glory. 31 And he shall send his angels with a great sound of a trumpet, and they shall gather together his elect from the four winds, from one end of heaven to the other.	• Will this 'coming' be sudden as or gradual and progressive? • Will this coming be secretly as a thief? • Who are these groups of elect be? • When will they be gathered • Will this group experience tribulation?

Matthew	16:27 For the Son of man shall come in the glory of his Father with his angels; and then he shall reward every man according to his works.	Is this the same as coming as a thief?
Matthew	23:39 For I say unto you, Ye shall not see me henceforth, till ye shall say, Blessed is he that cometh in the name of the Lord.	Is this the same as coming as a thief?
Matthew	24:30 And then shall appear the sign of the Son of man in heaven: and then shall all the tribes of the earth mourn, and they shall see the Son of man coming in the clouds of heaven with power and great glory.	Is this the same as coming as a thief?
Matthew	26:64 Jesus saith unto him, Thou hast said: nevertheless I say unto you, Hereafter shall ye see the Son of man sitting on the right hand of power, and coming in the clouds of heaven.	Is this the same as coming as a thief?
Mark	8:38 Whosoever therefore shall be ashamed of me and of my words in this adulterous and sinful generation; of him also shall the Son of man be ashamed, when he cometh in the glory of his Father with the holy angels.	Is this the same as coming as a thief?

Chapter 8

REASONS FOR RAPTURE:

The Rapture of the Saints, will lead to many things thereafter. This event will usher in a more intimate relation between Christ and His Bride –The chosen few, from the Church.

The Purpose of the Rapture are many, but a few are listed below.

A Purpose
- To have the Marriage between the Bridegroom and His Bride
- To reward the Saints
- To escape the wrath of king of fierce countenance, the Anti Christ
- To escape extremely terrible cataclysmic events on earth
- To join God's powerful army, coming back to conquer the inhabitants and the kings of the earth.
- To unite God's family, from the time of antiquity to now, under one umbrella

B Scriptural References

Purpose	References
Marriage	Let us be glad and rejoice, and give honour to him: for the marriage of the Lamb is come, and his wife hath made herself ready. Rev 19:7
To give rewards	For we must all appear before the judgment seat of Christ; that every one may receive the things done in his body, according to that he hath done, whether it be good or bad. 2 Cor 5:10

To escape the wrath of Anti Christ	"...; and when he shall have accomplished to scatter the power of the holy people, all these things shall be finished Daniel 12:7
Escape cataclysmic events	"And there shall be signs in the sun, and in the moon, and in the stars; and upon the earth distress of nations, with perplexity; the sea and the waves roaring; 21:26 Men's hearts failing them for fear, and for looking after those things which are coming on the earth: for the powers of heaven shall be shaken" Luke 21:25
To join God's powerful army	And the kings of the earth, and the great men, and the rich men, and the chief captains, and the mighty men, and every bondman, and every free man, hid themselves in the dens and in the rocks of the mountains; 6:16 And said to the mountains and rocks, Fall on us, and hide us from the face of him that sitteth on the throne, and from the wrath of the Lamb: 6:17 For the great day of his wrath is come; and who shall be able to stand? Rev 6:15
To unite God's family under one umbrella	And other sheep I have, which are not of this fold: them also I must bring, and they shall hear my voice; and there shall be one fold, and one shepherd. John 10:16

The Rescue from God's wrath, Tribulation;

"And I heard another voice from heaven, saying, Come out of her, my people, that ye be not partakers of her sins, and that ye receive not of her plagues."

Revelation 18:4

Chapter 9

THE SAFETY OF THE BRIDE, AND OTHER SAINTS

A 'Accounted worthy' to escape

Specifically, God states in His word that all who are 'accounted worthy' will be delivered during the Tribulation. That is, all who, at the time of Rapture, are in good standing, or whose names are not expunged or blotted out from the book of life, at the time of rescue operation.

Details of Biblical references will be given later in the book.

Found below are just a few of the Biblical EVIDENCES

B   All whose names are in the book of life will be delivered before the time of great trouble – the great Tribulation.Daniel 12:1

C   The phases of rescue plans for Saints will be finished before the Anti-Christ is ready to strike. Daniel 12:6-7

D   The New Jerusalem, the hiding place for the Bride, spotted coming down. Revelation 21:2

E   The Bride, hidden on a great and high mountain before the seven plagues is poured on the earth. Revelation 21:9

F   Holy Saints ordered out of Babylon - the sinful Earth, before the Tribulation. Revelation 18:4

G   The faithful kept out of the hour of trial – the great Tribulation Revelation 3:10

H   The escapee Saints, spotted on glassy sea

Before the seven angels proceed to the Saints were seen located on a glassy sea. The question then is,

- Who are these Saints?
- When did they escape from the Earth?
- By what means were they rescued from the Earth?

The scripture below, is a clear-cut case of Rapture and speaks for itself Revelation 15:2 -8

I   Summary of the deliverance plans in the book of Daniel and Revelation

The following scriptural snapshots are ample evidences of deliverance before the Tribulation and, hence, the Rapture.

1   Deliverance for the righteous at the time of Tribulation
Daniel 12:1

2   Deliverance will be in phases

At the time the Anti Christ accomplishes his plans to destroy God's children; the entire deliverance process will be finished. From the phrase "all these things shall be finished." As captured In Daniel 12:7, it means the deliverance process begun at an earlier time, and finished at the time of the Anti Christ was just ready to strike at the Saints. Daniel 12:7

3   The bride hidden in the New Jerusalem

A special Bridal chamber, a place of safety and comfort, in the New Jerusalem will be the camp, where the Bride of Christ will be kept, as the Tribulation proceeds on the Earth. Revelation 21:2

4   The bride hidden in a safe place, before the last 7 plagues – safety guaranteed

Before the seven last plagues were poured, an assurance was given to st John that the Bride, the Lamb's wife is safe. "The safety of the Bride is sure and guaranteed, totally out of danger of experiencing the tribulation," the angel seems to imply.

It is for the above reason, the angel said; "…Come hither, I will shew thee the bride, the Lamb's wife…"

The Full text of Revelation 21:9-10, is captured below.
"…., Come hither, I will shew thee the bride, the Lamb's wife. 21:10 And he carried me away in the spirit to a great and high mountain, and shewed me that great city, the holy Jerusalem, descending out of heaven from God," Revelation 21:9

5   God's Rescue command to His people Before the Tribulation

The following scripture is a further evidence of pre-Tribulation Rapture for the True Saints of God;

"And I heard another voice from heaven, saying, Come out of her, my people, that ye be not partakers of her sins, and that ye receive not of her plagues." Revelation 18:4

There is very vital information in the above scripture.
They are"
- "Come out of her, my people"
- "that ye be not partakers of her sins"
- "that ye receive not of her plagues"

The 'her' here refers to the Earth, Babylon. "My people" refers to God's people at the time of rescue or deliverance. This means, the Bride will be snatched out with a command from God himself. Else, they will also taste of the plagues upon the Earth. The wrath of God's punishment will be on the unrepentant, and not on the repentant.

6   Christ himself gives assurance of deliverance to the faithful followers.

This assurance is only for those 'accounted worthy', that is, those in good standing with Him at the time of rescue operation. Revelation 3:10
Note that;
- Those in good standing are said to have kept the "word of my patience,"
- The "hour of temptation" is the tribulation
- The Tribulation "shall come upon all the world"

- The Tribulation will come upon the entire world, "to try them that dwell upon the earth"; not those 'accounted worthy' to escape all these.
- Those tried here those given the last chance to repent and stand for Christ, in the face of pain and anguish, or remain defiant and be damned.
- This may include potential wedding guest, the nation of Israel, and the Tribulation Saints. Hence, Jesus said

"And in the latter time of their kingdom, when the transgressors are come to the full, a king of fierce countenance, and understanding dark sentences, shall stand up." Daniel 8:23

Chapter 10

THE ANTI-CHRIST -THE BEAST

A   The Peace Covenant in Daniel's 70th week

In the last 7 years of the world, that is, the 70th week of Prophet Daniel will emerge a strange person. This person is Satan's counterfeit Messiah, a false Savior of the world, a supposed 'peace-maker', a man that will project himself, initially, as a man of peace! But later, this 'man of peace' will cause all that dwell on the world to declare allegiance him, and for that matter to Satan, instead of the True God, thereby leading multitudes astray, as hinted in the book of Daniel and Revelation, and other scriptures.

The book of Daniel refers to this strange person, as a 'man of fierce countenance', whilst the book of revelation calls him the beast with number 666.

However, in the Epistles of the Apostles, he is called the Anti-Christ. This same man shall enter into a 7year peace treaty with Israel, only to display his true character 3 ½ years later, setting up an image of Satan that must be worshipped, as indicated in Daniel 9:27..... "And he shall confirm the covenant with many for one week: and in the midst of the week he shall cause the sacrifice and the oblation to cease, and for the overspreading of abominations he shall make it desolate, even until the consummation, and that determined shall be poured upon the desolate" Daniel 9:27

This 'man of peace' shall be endorsed by other powerful nations of the world, and will have policies that are Ant–Christ, powerfully persecuting the true Children of God, as in Daniel 8:23; ..."And in the latter time of their kingdom, when the transgressors are come to the full, a king of fierce countenance, and understanding dark sentences, shall stand up. ….." Daniel 8:23

B Some of the names and titles of the Anti-Christ!

In the scriptures, this strange fellow has several names and titles. Among them are;

• The king of Babylon – Is 14:4 • The son of perdition –2 Thessalonians 2:3 • The beast – Rev 13 :1 • The willful king – Dan 11:36 • The vile person – Dan 11:21 • The prince that shall come – Dan 9:26	• The little horn – Dan 7:8 • The man of sin – 2 Thessalonians 2:3 • The Assyrians – Is 10:5-12 • The spoiler – Is 16:4-5 • The king of fierce countenance – Dan 8:23 • The king of the north – Dan11:36-45

C Some of the major Characteristic of the Anti- Christ

1. He shall set up an image and demand worship
2. He shall seek to wage war on God's Son, Jesus Christ
3. He shall try to initiate the inhabitants of the Earth, into Satanic worship
4. He shall have intense hatred for God's True Children
5. He shall have a number 666, a mark, or name as his trade mark
6. He shall enter into a 7-year peace treaty, or covenant, with Israel
7. He shall emerge as a man of Peace
8. He shall set up and abomination and demand worship
9. He shall cause all to receive a special mark, a mark called the mark of the beast
10. He shall break the agreement in the middle of the 7-year period
11. He shall blaspheme the almighty God
12. He shall have a worldwide approval by powerful nations
13. He shall be very powerful and mighty
14. He shall be supported by false prophets of Christ, his agents.
15. These false prophets of Christ will be used as a major strategy of Satan to deceive many unknowingly, to receive the mark of the beast.

D The mark of the Beast – A sign of loyalty to Satan

The sign of loyalty to the Beast, and hence Satan

During the great Tribulation, the greatest danger that the inhabitants of planet Earth will be faced with is the untold pressure to declare loyalty to the Beast, that is, the Anti Christ.

The system in place will trap many to accept. This mark is called the mark of the Beast. All the Inhabitants of the Earth will be caught between the rock and the hard places. Why? Without the mark, there can be neither buying nor selling.

Furthermore, refusal to receive the mark, or worship the Beast, means instant death, through beheading.

On the other hand, receiving the mark, too, automatically guarantees a person's entrance into the LAKE OF FIRE.
Revelation 13:15

Hence, the greatest obstacle to survival on planet earth, during the tribulation, will be disloyalty to the Beast – the Anti Christ. Note: Rejection of any of this means instant death.
• The mark of the Beast
• Name of the beast
• The number of his name. - 666
• Worship of the Beast

On the other hand, the acceptance of any of the above IRREVERSIBILY MAKES YOU AN ENEMY OF GOD! Acceptance of any of the above gives you an automatic qualification into the LAKE OF FIRE, absolutely no chance whatsoever of REVERSAL of the automatic eternal doom.

E Rejection of the mark of the beast, a must - extremely important warning:
Rejection of the mark of the beast, and accepting Christ during the Tribulation, means declaration of loyalty to God. This could mean death; but finally enables a person to escape HELL FIRE, attracting a reward of ruling with Christ on the Earth for thousand years, after Christ returns to the Earth, gloriously.

"And the third angel followed them, saying with a loud voice, If any man worship the beast and his image, and receive his mark in his forehead, or in his hand, 14:10 The same shall drink of the wine of the wrath of God, which is poured out without mixture into the cup of his indignation; and he shall be tormented with fire and brimstone in the presence of the holy angels, and in the presence of the Lamb:." Revelation 14:9 -10

F   Two-fold Penalty for rejecting the mark of the beast
Every inhabitant of the Earth, during the great Tribulation, will be caught between the rock and the hard places. Receiving the mark, gives a person, automatically, an irreversible ticket to the LAKE OF FIRE, as already mentioned above. Not receiving it also attracts ALL of the following punishment.
- Inability to buy or sell anything on the planet Earth
- Instant Beheading

Failure to be well-positioned in Christ, for Rapture, puts a person in an extremely terrible and difficult situation during the Great Tribulation. For his reason,

Jesus Christ said in Luke 21:36
"Watch ye therefore, and pray always, that ye may be accounted worthy to escape all these things that shall come to pass, and to stand before the Son of man" Luke 21:36

There will be no special protection for Saints still on Earth, during this period, as indicated in the following scripture. The Beast will have full power over everyone, whether Christian or not, as indicated below.

Revelation 13:7 – 18, 14:9-13, Revelation 16:1-2
"And it was given unto him to make war with the saints, and to overcome them: and power was given him over all kindreds, and tongues, and nations. 13:8 And all that dwell upon the earth shall worship him, whose names are not written in the book of life of the Lamb slain from the foundation of the world. 13:9 If any man have an ear, let him hear. ... . 13:18 Here is wisdom. Let him that hath understanding count the number of the beast: for it is the number of a man; and his number is Six hundred threescore and six". Revelation 13:7 – 18

G Highlights of Revelation 13:7 – 18, 14:9-13, 16:1-2, 20:4 -5

- The Beast will have power to overcome Saints on the Earth
  …" Revelation 13:7
- All people, whose names are not in the book, will end up worshiping the Beast " Revelation 13:8
- Many will be deceived, using miracles, causing them to worship the Beast…". Revelation 13:14
- Refusal to worship the Beast, means instant death. Revelation 13:15
- Without a special identification number of the Anti Christ, there can be no baying or selling on the entire Earth.
  "…And that no man might buy or sell, save he that had the mark, or the name of the beast, or the number of his name…." Revelation 13:17
- Any form of loyalty to the Beast qualifies you for the lake of fire
  Revelation 14:9
- The first plague is for the Beast and those who worshipped the Beast, the Anti – Christ.
- Revelation 16:1 Saints beheaded for the witness of Jesus – no special protection at this time
- The beheaded Saint reigned with Christ for 1000years
  Revelation 20:4-5

H Judgment of the Beast - Revelation 16:2 Revelation 16:2
Revelation 16:10

"…: and the government shall be upon his shoulder: and his name shall be called Wonderful, Counsellor, The mighty God, The everlasting Father, The Prince of Peace" Isaiah 9:6

Chapter 11

THE DANGERS FALSE PROPHETS POSE TO UNSUSPECTING SOULS

A Counterfeits in God's house

For almost every good thing on earth, there is a corresponding counterfeit, and spiritual things are no exception. A typical example is the Prophetic Ministry. Satan too has his own counterfeit, called the false prophets. Their ultimate agenda is to entice unsuspecting souls, and lead them astray.

Jesus Christ Said in Matthew 24:11
"And many false prophets shall rise, and shall deceive many."
Matthew 24:11

But, this does not mean the entire prophetic Ministry should be shunned or ignored. Just as the circulation of counterfeit money does not prevent us from using money, so we also the Prophetic Ministry should not be shunned because of false prophets. Instead, we need to be become more careful, to distinguish between the wheat from the tares.

As the prophetic ministry grows, certainly, the infiltration of false prophets into God's house will also become more prevalent. This calls for more vigilance as indicated in 1 Peter 5:8;

Our Lord Jesus Christ warned that false prophets will come into the fold, as wolves dressed in sheep's clothing, especially in the end-time.

B Who is a false prophet?

During the Tribulation, and the great Tribulation period, false Prophet will come to the aid of the Antichrist, to speed up the doom of multitudes.

Hence, prior to any further discussion, it is important to identify who a false prophet is, for there are many in the world today.

False prophets can be recognized by their lack of adherence to Scriptural truth. Whenever a doctrine that has no Scriptural basis is persistently presented as truth, then the person is a false prophet or teacher. A message may be spiced up with soothing words that are sweet to hear, yet the message may not be of God. It may be coming from the preacher himself, or Satan. Often it may be based upon his personal lusts, and biases, all intended to achieve a specific goal. Jesus Christ warned in Matthew 7:15-20: "Beware of false prophets ..."

Highlights,
- False prophets come as wolves in sheep's clothing
- False prophets operate as predators
- Both genuine Prophets and false prophets are to be known by their fruits.

C   Deception and seduction of false prophets
The ability to reach large groups of people, seduce them, often offering them some type hope in a crisis situation, is the key strategy.

Amazingly, some of these practitioners of evil doctrine are so gifted. False prophets possess gift capable of trapping even professing Christians, making them part of their flocks, and leading such into perdition. For this reason,

Jesus Christ said in Matthew 24:24:
".For there shall arise false Christ(s), and false prophets, and shall shew great signs and wonders; insomuch that, if it were possible, they shall deceive the very elect."

"For false Christ(s), and false prophets shall rise, ..." Mark 13:22-23:
Currently, the world is filled with many antichrists and false prophets. However, in the Tribulation, two satanic traps will be most prominent, which that will surpass all previous wickedness.

These are;

• The Antichrist himself – the beast
• The False Prophets

D   Strategy to be employed by false Prophets!

The role of false prophets will be to serve as eternal death traps for many souls; before and during the tribulation.

The role of the false prophets is to redirect the human traffic to the Beast. The focal strategy of these false prophets will be to attract souls into their fold, initiate them, and cause them to declare allegiance to the Anti-Christ, by causing them to receive the mark of the beast, or worship the beast, using deceptions.

To facilitate, or fast track, the achievement of their goal, satanically inspired problem may increase in the End time, creating the need for solution. As part of their world vision, the key strategy of the Anti Christ will be decentralized his activities, worldwide, using his agents, the false prophets, to facilitate quick recruitment into his fold, and given the mark of the beast – the path of eternal perdition.

"And through his policy also he shall cause craft to prosper in his hand; and he shall magnify himself in his heart, and by peace shall destroy many: he shall also stand up against the Prince of princes; but he shall be broken without hand" Daniel 8:25

Full text of Matthew 24:11, Revelation 16:13-14, 19:19-20, 20:10
"..And many false prophets shall rise, and shall deceive many."
Jesus said in Matthew 24:11;

E   A special revelation and case Study - the traps of false prophets in the end time

Found below is a verbatim revelation given to sister.
Note: This experience of the sister, immediately below, is copied and pasted unedited.

"I saw myself and another sister walking side by side jesting normally.

A man was walking at the other side; suddenly the man turned and said the rapture has just taken place 30 seconds ago, and looking at the time It was 1.00.30s AM. The man proceeded by saying go in the left direction you will find other Christians there, do not go in the right direction. They are taking the mark already. Go now I give you one minute.. I asked him what about you? He turned and said I am the antichrist who has lived in your midst for so long waiting for this day. I was confused but my spirit said run, my son run. We ran and on covering some distance. I turned back; lo and behold the man we left has turned to the antichrist. We kept running and saw many other people running as well. We got to a very large auditorium too large to be described and behold multitudes of Christians... Brethren it was a terrifying experience. People of high standing with God, Prominent men and women of God, loved ones and friends! I couldn't comprehend this so I screamed, all of us, God what happened?

The Lord now took me in the spirit to five churches:
In a predominant church of one tribe, I saw the pastors announcing that the rapture has just taken place and that people should start receiving the mark right there in the church that this will substitute the said beast mark and enable them to buy and sell. Brethren, what made me weep was that the innocent and ignorant members started receiving this mark not knowing it was actually the mark of the beast.

The Lord then said all these pastors are agents of the beast who has been ordained to mislead the people and who already has the beast mark before his manifestation, and I saw marks on the right arm of all these pastors. A brother who was fortunate to see who to call him to start running down to the place where all other Christians are was shot in the leg as he was about climbing the top of the Christian's hide out.

Then the Lord took me again to another church where the pastors were just speaking of the good things of the scripture and didn't talk about the second coming of Christ and warn the people of the wages of sin. The irony of it was that all these pastors and their members were left behind.
Then I saw another church where people did really emphasize the coming but all the people didn't go as a result of the hidden sins which weren't

known to man and they had not counted as sin. I wept bitterly because this was a church where holiness was professed and held in high esteem.

I saw another church where people concentrated mainly on attacking demons and where the true word was also preached but the people also didn't go due to malice and lack of spiritual concentration. I saw yet another church where the people were actively involved in preaching the word and talking about the second coming, however these people did not go. The whole lot was full of hypocrites who disguise themselves in shepherd's clothes. I was then taken back to the place where the multitude were and then I saw that the people of the beast came and Christians started scrambling for safety. Brethren it was a terrifying experience. Women forgot their children, husbands their wives. We ran and got to another place of hiding but the surprising thing which should make all shiver was that the population was now so small that it was easy for every one to identify each other as family and friends started pairing up. The Lord then said others have received the mark.

Brethren the people I saw made me weep uncontrollably. Prominent men of God all over the world, Christians and loved ones! I now asked the LORD why all these one and God showed me different people and men of God saying: this man was perfect with me until 2 hours ago. That other had a small portion of his heart released to the devil. That other brother was too occupied with the things of the world in terms of land and property acquisition that they took over his life. That other one, I gave him a mandate to pay a certain portion of money to the church and he procrastinated it till now: sin of disobedience.

That other so much loves his cheque book than his life. You can even see that he has his cheque book with him I wonder what he can buy with the money now: hope you know they are no more his. I wept because so many little things which we humans don't count were counted by God. I now spoke with a confused voice, help us Lord.

The Lord then said all these things which have been happening on earth have all been pointing to the end but despite all this, my people do not take heed. I am giving the last warning. Consecrate your hearts to me, my people.

The trumpet would have been blown one hour ago, but I pleaded with my father. However, I can plead no further. The trumpet is already in the mouths of the Angels ready to be blown.

SO PREPARE YE THY WAYS OH MY PEOPLE.
Tell my people to read Matthew 16:3. And warn all the ministers who has gone in the ways of BAAL.

THIS IS TRUE AND BELIEVE IT OR NOT THE RAPTURE IS AT HAND. HELL AND HEAVEN ARE REAL..REPENT YE MY BRETHREN.

PLS HELP ME OUT BY SPREADING THIS WORD TO ALL YOU KNOW." The end of QUOTE

F Warning for false prophets and teachers
The Bible has strong warnings for false prophets and teachers.

God's word says in Ezekiel 13:1-12;
"And the word of the LORD came unto me, saying, 13:2 Son of man, prophesy against the prophets of Israel that prophesy, and say thou unto them that prophesy out of their own hearts, Hear ye the word of the LORD; 13:3 … 13:8 Therefore thus saith the Lord GOD; Because ye have spoken vanity, and seen lies, therefore, behold, I am against you, saith the Lord GOD. 13:9 And mine hand shall be upon the prophets that see vanity, and that divine lies: they shall not be in the assembly of my people, neither shall they be written in the writing of the house of Israel, neither shall they enter into the land of Israel; and ye shall know that I am the Lord GOD.

Furthermore God's word says in Jeremiah 6:13 -15
"For from the least of them even unto the greatest of them every one is given to covetousness; and from the prophet even unto the priest every

one dealeth falsely. 6:14 They have healed also the hurt of the daughter of my people slightly, saying, Peace, peace; when there is no peace. 6:15 Were they ashamed when they had committed abomination? nay, they were not at all ashamed, neither could they blush: therefore they shall fall among them that fall: at the time that I visit them they shall be cast down, saith the LORD". Jeremiah 6:13-15

"Then said the LORD unto me, Pray not for this people for their good. 14:12 When they fast, I will not hear their cry; and when they offer burnt offering and an oblation, I will not accept them: but I will consume them by the sword, and by the famine, and by the pestilence.

14:13 Then said I, Ah, Lord GOD! behold, the prophets say unto them, Ye shall not see the sword, neither shall ye have famine; but I will give you assured peace in this place. ....." Jeremiah 14:11-16

Highlights of Matthew 24:11, Revelation 16:13-14, 19:19-20, 20:10
- Many false prophets shall arise
- Many shall be lead astray
- Many will work miracles using the spirit of devils
- The kings of the earth will be deceived by evil spirits
- The kings of the earth will gathered to the battle of Armageddon
- The beast and kings of the earth shall make war with Our Lord Jesus Christ
- The beast and kings of the earth shall be taken captured
- The beast, false prophets and the kings of the earth shall be thrown into

" Alas! for that day is great, so that none is like it: it is even the time of Jacob's trouble; but he shall be saved out of it" Jeremiah 30:7,

Chapter 12

THE RAPTURE WINDOWS OF ESCAPE AT THE END TIME

A   Categories of Saints during Christ's earthly Ministry

On the basis of God's word, as stated earlier in this book, it is certain that there are different categories of Saints of God. Each of these categories has different levels of position in relation Christ. For instance, during our Lord Jesus Christ's earthly ministry, although His followers were all called his disciples, it s indisputable fact that within the big family, called his disciples, were different categories of disciples.

The hierarchy of LOVE for His disciples, during his Earthly ministry, beginning from the inner core to the outer core may be listed as follows. They are;

- Category 1   John, the beloved
- Category 2   Peter, James and John
- Category 3   The twelve disciples, minus 1
- Category 4   The seventy disciples
- Category 5   The rest of the disciples

B   Category depends on the bond of Love and faithfulness

The level of bond, or love, that exist between Christ and each category determines the closeness of the relationship. For instance, st John had the privilege of receiving the book of revelation for Christ to the entire Church. The depth of revelations he received was not given to other disciples.

Peter, James and John had a rare privilege of seeing the transfiguration of Christ, and beheld Christ in His glory with Moses and the Elijah etc

Also, the core messages, captured in the Gospel, were received first hand by the 12 disciples, etc. Out of these 12 disciples, a few were privileged to pen down the detail account of His Earthly Ministry.

C Categorization of Saints in the Church in the End Time

So also, although, our Lord Jesus Christ loves the entirety of His body, called the body of Christ, or the Children of God, or the Church, there are different categories of Saints within His Church.

i Key categories of Saints

Some of the key categories identified in the book of revelation are;

Category 1:	The Bride	Rev 21:9
Category 2:	The wedding guest	Rev 19:9
Category 3:	The Tribulation Saints	Rev 7:14
Category 4:	The Beheaded Saints	Rev 20:4

The other categories are;
- The old Testament Saints   Heb 11:32-39
- The 144,000 Jewish Evangelist   Rev 7:4
- The remnants of nation of Israel   Romans 9:27 Etc

D Resurrection and Departure from the Earth of the dead Saints

The first category of all Saints that will be 'air-lifted', during the Rapture, is the dead in Christ as indicated in 1 Thessalonians 4:16.. "For the Lord himself shall descend from heaven with a shout, with the voice of the archangel, and with the trump of God: and the dead in Christ shall rise first: 4:17 Then we which are alive and remain shall be caught up together with them in the clouds, to meet the Lord in the air: and so shall we ever be with the Lord. 4:18 Wherefore comfort one another with these words." 1 Thessalonians 4:16

E Root cause of conflicting opinion on Rapture

The first category of the living Saints, that will be 'air-lifted', during the Rapture, is the Bride of Christ, followed by the wedding guest, then Tribulation Saints, then the resurrection of the Beheaded Saints. The Timing for each varies. This is the root cause of so much confusion, with regard to conflict of opinion, over the End Time events.

Whilst some Christians hold the view of pre-Tribulation is the correct one, others believe that mid-Tribulation, or pre-wrath, or post –Tribulation is the correct End Time doctrine.

For each of the above, scriptures are pin pointed in an effort to justify the opinion. Depending on where you are looking at the issue from, whether you referring to the Bride, the wedding guest, Tribulation Saints, or the Beheaded Saints, there is some element of truth in each; hence no need to out-rightly condemn the other.

F   Departure from the Earth of the living Saints
   i   The choice of Saints – Many are called but few chosen of course, you might have read or come across this popular passage, that is, Matthew 22:14; "For many are called, but few are chosen".

Have you ever pondered over it; and then asked yourself, when or where exactly does this scripture become applicable, or when does this scripture come into force, in the body of Christ?

Many are indeed "translated from darkness to light, that is called from darkness to light, as indicated in Colossians 1:12,

Colossians 1:12, states;
"Giving thanks unto the Father, which hath made us meet to be partakers of the inheritance of the saints in light: 1:13 Who hath delivered us from the power of darkness, and hath translated us into the kingdom of his dear Son:" Colossians 1:12

Yes, "For many are called, but few are chosen". Matthew 22:14;
Please, try and answer the following questions;
•   For what purpose are the few chosen?
•   When are they Chosen?
•   What are chosen for?
•   Where are chosen to?

ii   The Window for The departure of the Bride   Timing for the
     1'airlift' — pre-tribulation
     On the basis of the earlier discussion, under 'scenarios for
     Rapture', only scenarios 5 and 6 are consistent with the scriptures.
     Hence, from these two scenarios, the Bride will be 'air-lifted' at
     least 45 days before, but not more than 1335 days before, the
     beginning of the 7-year Tribulation, as shown below;

5. Scenario 5
*   Let us assume the 1335 days mentioned in Daniel 12, starts on the 45th
    day before the start of the tribulation

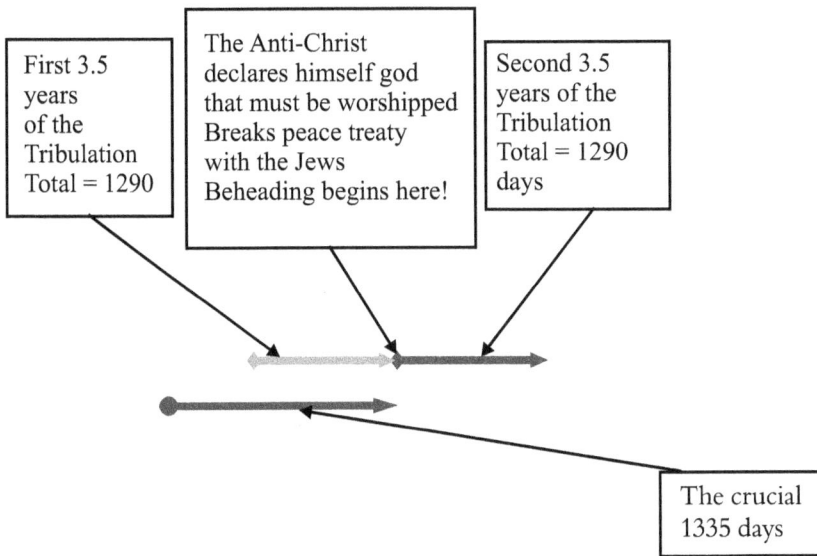

| First 3.5 years of the Tribulation Total = 1290 | The Anti-Christ declares himself god that must be worshipped Breaks peace treaty with the Jews Beheading begins here! | Second 3.5 years of the Tribulation Total = 1290 days |

The crucial 1335 days

Remarks:
From this scenario, it means the "blessed" is he who "waiteth" and
"cometh", do so $1335 - (45+1290) = 0$ days $=$ the start of the mid-
Tribulation. The element of surprise, greatly exist here.
This means the following are all boxed together to suffer the same fate –
that is, beheading. They are;
   xii. The beheaded Saints

6. Scenario 6

Let us assume the 1335 days starts more than 45 days before the tribulation. Example 50 days

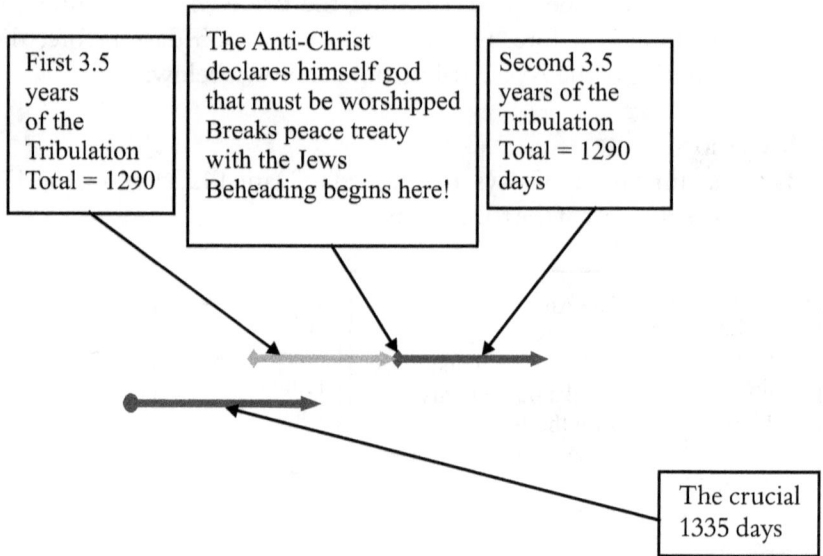

```
┌─────────────┐   ┌──────────────────────┐   ┌──────────────┐
│ First 3.5   │   │ The Anti-Christ      │   │ Second 3.5   │
│ years       │   │ declares himself god │   │ years of the │
│ of the      │   │ that must be worshipped│ │ Tribulation  │
│ Tribulation │   │ Breaks peace treaty  │   │ Total = 1290 │
│ Total = 1290│   │ with the Jews        │   │ days         │
│             │   │ Beheading begins here!│  │              │
└─────────────┘   └──────────────────────┘   └──────────────┘
```

┌──────────────┐
│ The crucial │
│ 1335 days   │
└──────────────┘

Remarks:

From this scenario, it means the "blessed" is he who "waiteth" and "cometh", do so 1335 – (50 + 1290) = 5 days before the start of the mid-Tribulation. The element of surprise, greatly exist here.

This means the tribulation saints clearly escape possibility of beheading. But the following resurrect later, that is,
   a.   The Tribulation Saints
   b.   The beheaded Saints

iii; Window for The departure of the and Tribulation Saints The 2nd 'air lift': mid – tribulation.

After the first major event on Earth, which could be no other event other than Rapture of the Bride, there will be 1335 days time lag for occurrence of the next major event.

From Daniel 12:12
"Blessed is he that waiteth, and cometh to the thousand three hundred and five and thirty days." Daniel12:12

In effect, the timing of he departure of this group, within the first half of the Tribulation, depends on when the Bride is "air-lifted", that is, when the Bride experience the 'Rapture'.

Of course, this will be the most anxious and agonizing moment in the life this group of Saints. There may be weeping and gnashing if teeth for the left behind, unsure about their fate.

Shifting the *crucial 1335 days* bar to the left reduces the length of time they will spend in the Tribulation period, and vice versa.

Hence, the earlier the Bride departs the better for this group. But the departure must be within the first half of the Tribulation, that is, the first 1290 days, to avoid the second half, the danger zone then the mark of the beast is introduced:

iv;   The Resurrection of the Beheaded Saints – post Tribulation
The window for the resurrection of this group of Saints is immediately after the Tribulation, when Christ appears gloriously. This could include the Saints that miraculously may have survived.

Closely monitoring Global events, in the light of scripture, it is becoming increasingly clear that the world is entering a crucial phase; a momentous event is fast approaching. To no avail, some may try to wish this away. Yes, the <u>SECOND COMING OF CHRIST</u> is fast approaching! It must concern ALL PEOPLE, both BELIEVERS and UNBELIEVERS. To be an IGNORAMUS, certainly is an unwise choice.

This part of this book, gives:
[a]   Some insight about His 2nd coming
[b]   A few cautions to everyone, especially all who, supposedly, are Disciples of Christ!

HIS SECOND COMING HAS 2 ASPECTS;
<u>EVENT 1</u>: Disappearance - Rapture -This will be done SECRETLY.
<u>EVENT 2</u>: appearance, physical, of Christ in the sky! This will be done publicly; occurring openly for every eye on earth to see him.

Jesus said
"And take heed to yourselves, lest at any time your hearts be overcharged with surfeiting, and drunkenness, AND CARES OF THIS LIFE, AND SO THAT DAY COME UPON YOU UNAWARES"
Luke 21:34

Chapter 13

RAPTURE - READINESS:
GENERAL GUIDELINES

A   Many are called, but few are chosen
In the light of the issues discussed in this book so far, please, ponder over the scripture below, that is, Matthew 22: 14, and answer the important questions thereafter

"For many are called, but few are chosen" Matthew 22: 14
Important question:
In all aspects of Christian life or Church age, in your candid opinion;
* Who are those referred to as, "For many are called…?"
* Who are those referred to as, "but few are chosen …?"
* When exactly, or at what stage, do you think Matthew 22: 14 will become applicable, throughout the entire Church age?
* What exact message, in your opinion, is Christ seeking to send to Christians, worldwide?

Please, be very, very honest and specific, in your attempt to find accurate answers to the questions above.

Our Lord Jesus Christ is emphatically saying there is a category called the "chosen few".
* Who are they?
* When will they be Chosen?
* Where will they be chosen to?
* For what purpose will they be chosen?

Again, Jesus declared in Luke 13: 24
"Strive to enter in at the strait gate: for many, I say unto you, will seek to
enter in, and shall not be able," Luke 13: 24

In effect, do not take the messages captured below lightly.
Ensure you PLUNGE your ENTIRE LIFE into Christ. Be a
'RAPTUREABLE material'. Be among the chosen few.

In the light of the above revelation, the most important question every one
must be asking is; Lord, what must I do to be a RAPTURABLE material,
or be RAPTURE - READY?

B   Strategies for making others Rapture-ready –
GENERAL GUIDELINES
Found below are a few general guidelines. However, as an individual, in
addition to the following general guideline, God may be speaking to you in
specific way. Be sensitive to Him.
- You must be truly born again, accepting Christ as your Lord and Savior
  John 3 : 16
- You must have intense love for Jesus Christ, through the power of the
  Holy Spirit. Psalm 2 : 12
- You must live in moment by moment obedience to the Lord's
  commandments. John 14 : 24
- Constantly ask for a pure heart, using the cleansing power of the blood
  of Christ. Matthew 5 : 8
- Share Christ with others, without being ashamed - VERY VITAL
  Luke 9:26 , Matthew 12 : 30b
- Have personal love for others, devoid of any trace of malice. Hebrews
  12 : 14
- Always be at peace with others Hebrews 12 : 14
- Live in daily HOLINESS and PURITY Hebrews 12 : 14
- Develop Love for things above more than things of this world. 1 John
  2 : 15
- Promote Kingdom business with cheerful heart and not with heavy
  heart. 2 Corinthians 9 : 7
- Have a Prayerful attitude, Luke 21: 36
- Allow God to speak to you, through his word. Psalm 119: 105
- Be sensitive and test every spirit that seeks to lure you, whether it is of

God. 1 John 4 : 1
- Do not sit on your God-given talents. Allow them to honor God and not the devil Matthew 25 : 18
- Avoid spiritual lukewarm ness, through fasting, sharing fellowship, etc Revelation 3 : 16
- Be child-like before God, but not childish. Matthew 18 : 3
- The BOTTOMLINE: "...Work out your own salvation with fear and trembling..." Phil" 2 : 12

D Strategies for making others Rapture-ready

Introduction:
Why is it necessary, and URGENT, for Christians to wake up and make others Rapture-ready? Because, our Lord commands us to do so, as captured in Ephesians 5:15 "See then that ye walk circumspectly, not as fools, but as wise, 5:16 Redeeming the time, because the days are evil. 5:17 Wherefore be ye not unwise, but understanding what the will of the Lord is." Ephesians 5:15

STEPS to make others rapture-ready
i   Brief outline
- Be sure you are Baptized with the Holy Ghost and with fire
- Prayer for a burden and compassion for lost Souls
- Make list of those who must be reached
- Identify various channels of communication
- Constantly hide everything about you in the blood of Jesus
- Bombard satanic barriers, and obstacles, to salivation.
- Present the Souls and the channels, to be used, to God
- Proceed to reach out to them
- Refuse to be diverted from focusing on Eternal life

ii   What does it mean to make others Rapture-ready?
It simply means making effort and ensuring that they genuinely born again, and are Heavenly minded, conscious of the need to always have their garments undefiled; living and working faithfully for God . For you to be able to achieve this, the above outlines are vital and are further explained as follows;

iii   Be sure you are Baptized with the Holy Ghost and fire

Without the power of the Holy Ghost, trying to reach others for Christ is a non-starter. This is vital because, salvation is not simply and intellectual exercise, but a Divine surgical operation on a Soul by the Holy Ghost, and we are the vessels God uses to accomplish this operation.

For this reason, Jesus said in Acts 1:8

"But ye shall receive power, after that the Holy Ghost is come upon you: and ye shall be witnesses unto me both in Jerusalem, and in all Judaea, and in Samaria, and unto the uttermost part of the earth." Acts 1:8

To receive this power, we must first tarry in our Jerusalem.

For this reason, Jesus said in Luke 24:49 "And, behold, I send the promise of my Father upon you: but tarry ye in the city of Jerusalem, until ye be endued with power from on high." Luke 24:49

ii   Prayer for a burden and compassion for lost Souls

There is a vital need to see things the way God see things. Many people may be financially very sound, rich materially and, perhaps, well placed in society, but spiritually wretched and heading for eternal doom. This is because they are far from the source of all life; not regenerated and have filthy garments.

Jesus sees Souls, with God's eye lenses as indicated in Matthew 9:36; "But when he saw the multitudes, he was moved with compassion on them, because they fainted, and were scattered abroad, as sheep having no shepherd." Matthew 9:36

iii   Make a list of those who must be reached

This is a list of Souls, starting from your own Jerusalem. That is, family members, love ones, fiends, acquaintances etc. It is good to have a world vision, but God's strategy, and for that matter, our strategy must be start from inside to outside;

Hence Jesus said in Acts 1:8

"…and ye shall be witnesses unto me both in Jerusalem, and in all Judaea, and in Samaria, and unto the uttermost part of the earth." Acts 1:8

iv Identify various channels of communication
Various channels of communication may be employed, but channels may depend on proximity, language understood, etc.
Examples of channels are;
*   One-on-one Evangelism
*   Distribution of Special Christian Tracts
*   Invitation to Church
*   Special message built into Email Auto-responder
*   Book recommendation
*   Crusade. Etc

v Constantly hide everything about you in the blood of Jesus
Be sure to make provision for counter-attack. Certainly, Satan will not allow his prisoners to be released without a fight. Make the Blood line of Jesus Christ your protection and be reminded of Ephesians 6:12; "...For we wrestle not against flesh and blood, but against principalities, against powers, against the rulers of the darkness of this world, against spiritual wickedness in high places. 6:13 ...." Ephesians 6:12

vi Bombard satanic barriers, and obstacles, to salivation.
Some people are locked up or tied to family evil alters, thrones, stools, witchcraft trees, etc. These may constitute major obstacles and need to be dealt with swiftly before any head way could be made. Remember that Souls are the 'precious goods' of satanic strongmen. You must first defeat the strong man before you can get access to the 'precious goods' Hence Jesus said; "...When a strong man armed keepeth his palace, his goods are in peace: 11:22 But when a stronger than he shall come upon him, and overcome him, he taketh from him all his armour wherein he trusted, and divideth his spoils." Luke 11:21

Again Jesus said; "...No man can enter into a strong man's house, and spoil his goods, except he will first bind the strong man; and then he will spoil his house." Mark 3:27

vii Present the Souls and the channels, to be used, to God
Ultimately, it is God that makes it possible for a Soul to come to Christ. Jesus Christ said;

"...No man can come to me, except the Father which hath sent me draw him: and I will raise him up at the last day." John 6:44

Therefore, it is necessary to petition Heaven concerning Souls, making intercession on their behalf.

Viii Proceed to reach out to them
Once all the necessary home work has been done, the next step is proceed in faith, and reach out, to communicate the good news to the unsaved, warning those who are already saved to keep their garments clean, to make them Rapture-able material when the 'thief' comes for His own.

ix Refuse to be diverted from focusing on Eternal life
Keep focus on your goal, and avoid allowing yourself to be dragged into unnecessary religious terrain.

Ask for wisdom from above, to know how to pedal questions, which are remotely packaged by Satan, intended to lure you away from the essential issues at stake, that is knowing Christ, being saved; thereby making the Rapture and ultimately going to Heaven. These are the essential issues; any other thing is a secondary matter.

Jesus said;

"Watch ye therefore: for ye know not when the master of the house cometh, at even, or at midnight, or at the cockcrowing, or in the morning: 13:36 Lest coming suddenly he find you sleeping." Mark 13:35

Chapter 14

VITAL BIBLICAL LESSONS

A Reason's why Rapture is no JOKE - CRUCIAL

Perhaps, the most important part of this entire book is this chapter. A person may choose to ignore vital warnings in life, but the one may be doing so, at his or her own peril. In this chapter, several evidences will be adduced to convince you why you must not ignore the warnings captured in this book, and for that matter, the crucial information captured in the entire Bible.

Jesus Christ said;
"...., and hold fast, and repent. If therefore thou shalt not watch, I will come on thee as a thief, and thou shalt not know what hour I will come upon thee" Revelation 3:3

This is a clear-cut case of Rapture-coming
Jesus Christ said;
"Behold, I come as a thief. Blessed is he that watcheth, and keepeth his garments, lest he walk naked, and they see his shame." Revelation 16:15

This is another clear cut case of Rapture-coming
From Genesis to Revelation, several warnings, prophesies, or promises are given. Many have already been fulfilled, or are about to be fulfilled. Listed below are just a few of such classic cases. Each of these has already been fulfilled, with the exception of the last one, which is just about to be fulfilled as warned

1. Abraham informed by God, of his descendants going into captivity in a foreign land. Genesis 15:13

2. God's promise of deliverance of Abraham's descendant. Exodus 15:14
3. God's warns of Jerusalem going into captivity for seventy years. Jeremiah 22:25
4. God's promises rebuilding of Jerusalem, and desolation of Babylon after seventy years. Jeremiah 25:12
5. God's promise a messiah will come. Daniel 9:25
6. Christ warning to the Jews of going to captivity in all nations. Luke 21:24
7. God's promise of reassembling the Jew from all countries. Jeremiah 16:14
8. Finally, Christ giving waning of His sudden return. RAPTURE, SOON TO HAPPEN

B Vital prophesies and their corresponding fulfillment

Event Number	Information/warning/ or prophesy GIVEN	Information / warning / or prophesy FULFILLED
1	"And he said unto Abram, Know of a surety that thy seed shall be a stranger in a land that is not theirs, and shall serve them; and they shall afflict them four hundred years." Genesis 15:13	"And Jacob rose up from Beer-sheba: and the sons of Israel carried Jacob their father, and their little ones, and their wives, in the wagons which Pharaoh had sent to carry him. 46:6 And they took their cattle, and their goods, which they had gotten in the land of Canaan, and came into Egypt, Jacob, and all his seed with him: 46:7 His sons, and his sons' sons with him, his daughters, and his sons' daughters, and all his seed brought he with him into Egypt.;" Genesis 46:5
2	"And also that nation, whom they shall serve, will I judge: and afterward shall they come out with great substance." Exodus 15:14	"And it came to pass at the end of the four hundred and thirty years, even the selfsame day it came to pass, that all the hosts of the LORD went out from the land of Egypt." Exodus 12:41

3	"And I will give thee into the hand of them that seek thy life, and into the hand of them whose face thou fearest, even into the hand of Nebuchadrezzar king of Babylon, and into the hand of the Chaldeans. 22:26 And I will cast thee out, and thy mother that bare thee, into another country, where ye were not born; and there shall ye die." Jeremiah 22:25	"In the ninth year of Zedekiah king of Judah, in the tenth month, came Nebuchadrezzar king of Babylon and all his army against Jerusalem, and they besieged it. 39:2 And in the eleventh year of Zedekiah, in the fourth month, the ninth day of the month, the city was broken up" Jeremiah 39:1
4	"And it shall come to pass, when seventy years are accomplished, that I will punish the king of Babylon, and that nation, saith the LORD, for their iniquity, and the land of the Chaldeans, and will make it perpetual desolation" Jeremiah 25:12	"In the first year of Cyrus the king the same Cyrus the king made a decree concerning the house of God at Jerusalem, Let the house be builded, the place where they offered sacrifices, and let the foundations thereof be strongly laid; the height thereof threescore cubits, and the breadth thereof threescore cubits;." Ezra 6:3
5	"Know therefore and understand, that from the going forth of the commandment to restore and to build Jerusalem unto the Messiah the Prince shall be seven weeks, and threescore and two weeks: the street shall be built again, and the wall, even in troublous times;." Daniel 9:25	"Now when Jesus was born in Bethlehem of Judaea in the days of Herod the king, behold, there came wise men from the east to Jerusalem." Matthew 2:1
6	"And they shall fall by the edge of the sword, and shall be led away captive into all	This took place 70 AD·

	nations: and Jerusalem shall be trodden down of the Gentiles, until the times of the Gentiles be fulfilled." Luke 21:24	
7	"Therefore, behold, the days come, saith the LORD, that it shall no more be said, The LORD liveth, that brought up the children of Israel out of the land of Egypt; 16:15 But, The LORD liveth, that brought up the children of Israel from the land of the north, and from all the lands whither he had driven them: and I will bring them again into their land that I gave unto their fathers.." Jeremiah 16:14	• This is still happening live. • Jew returning Home after almost 1930 years in various counties of the world
8	"In my Father's house are many mansions: if it were not so, I would have told you. I go to prepare a place for you. 14:3 And if I go and prepare a place for you, I will come again, and receive you unto myself; that where I am, there ye may be also." John 14:2	VERY SOON

Jesus said;

"And what I say unto you I say unto all, Watch." Mark 13:37

Chapter 15

SPIRITUAL WARFARE PRAYERS AGAINST ANTI-RAPTURE SPIRITS

JESUS CHRIST said in Luke 21:36;

"Watch ye therefore, and pray always, that ye may be accounted worthy to escape all these things that shall come to pass, and to stand before the Son of man." Luke 21:36

DECLARATION OF WAR AGAINST:
a. The Spirit of PISGAH
b. The Spirit of SLUMBER and LUKEWARMNESS
c. The Spirit of GARMENT DEFILEMENT
d. The Spirit of INSUFFICIENT OIL
e. The Spirit of SELFISHNESS

A   THE SPIRIT OF PISGAH
One of the most dramatic rescue operations ever recorded in history, was the liberation of the nation of Israel from Egypt, approx 3500 years ago.

Some of the highlights of that dramatic event are as follows;
* It was a whole nation in bondage, and rescued; not just an individual.
* It recorded a unique and visible interaction between God and man.
* It recorded God, revealing himself as JEHOVAH, for the first time. Ex 6:3

- It recorded dumbfounding wonders, sending shivers down the spine.
- Physical laws were set aside, making a way through water [the red sea]

However, the aftermath of that escape was full of drama. For instance, many PERISHED, due to unbelief. Also, almost all the initial key leaders could not make it to the Promised Land. Drama within drama! And, perhaps, the most astounding of this drama within drama was the inability of the MUCH REVERED MAN OF GOD, MOSES, to see "the land flowing with milk & honey". 'Rev.' Moses was GREAT, with outstanding credentials; Example;.

- He was the first person ever to know God as; I AM THAT I AM. This occurred in the burning bush.
- He was the first person ever to know God as Jehovah. Not even Abraham, Isaac and Jacob knew God as Jehovah;
- The rescue operation for the entire nation of Israel, already planned by God, was first revealed to him.
- By just raising his hand, the ENTIRE ARMY, of the then superpower, perished.
- He talked to God, mouth to mouth, on the mountain of FIRE & SMOKE.
- He is, perhaps, the only person in the Bible known to have fasted for two 40 days and two 40 night = 80 days and 80 nights.
- The earth opened its mouth, swallowed up those who 'just' murmured against him.
- He was the conduit or channel for presenting God's Ten Commandments to man on planet Earth.
- He was one of the first harbingers of Christ's 1ST coming to this earth.

BUT, in spite of all these extraordinary achievements, HE FAILED TO ARREST the SPIRIT OF PISGAH.

Question: What is the Spirit of PISGAH?
God's word said in Deut 3:26 "and the LORD said unto me [Moses], Let it suffice thee;. 3:27 "Get thee up into the TOP OF PISGAH, and lift up thine eyes westward, and northward, and southward, and eastward, and

behold it with thine eyes: for THOU SHALT NOT GO OVER THIS JORDAN."

REASON FOR NOT ENTERING THE PROMISED LAND:
He MADE ONE TRAGIC ERROR. With his rod, he struck the rock; DISOBEYING GOD'S COMMAND, to SPEAK TO THE ROCK. [Num 20:7-12]

THAT ROCK WAS CHRIST. [1Cor 10:4].
Hence, he saw the Promised Land, but DID NOT ENTER IT. THE SPIRIT OF PISGAH IS A WICKED SPIRIT IS THAT:

• Allows a person to see his Promised Land, without entering it.
• Causes an unpardonable error, at the crucial moment in ones life.
• Seeks to pitch a man, chosen by God, against his God and maker.
• Denies a man of reaping the fruits of his labour, after a hard work.
• Closely monitors a man's progress, only to strike at the last hour.
• Prefers to use physique, instead of prayer - speaking to the ROCK.
• Robs a man of his milk & honey - wealth, comfort, peace with God.

Scriptural References;
God's word said in Deut 9:18 "And I [Moses] fell down before the LORD, as at the first, forty days and forty nights: I did neither eat bread, nor drink water, because of all your sins which ye sinned, in doing wickedly in the sight of the LORD, to provoke him to anger."

God's word said in Exodus 6:2 ", I am the LORD:... 6:3 And I APPEARED UNTO ABRAHAM, UNTO ISAAC, AND UNTO JACOB, BY THE NAME OF GOD ALMIGHTY, BUT BY MY NAME JEHOVAH WAS I NOT KNOWN TO THEM."

God's word said in 1 Cor10:3 ": FOR THEY DRANK OF THAT SPIRITUAL ROCK THAT FOLLOWED THEM: AND THAT ROCK WAS CHRIST.

God's word said in Numbers 20:11 "And Moses lifted up his hand, and with his rod he smote the rock twice: and the water came out abundantly, and the congregation drank, and their beasts also. 20:12 And the LORD spake unto Moses and Aaron, <u>Because ye believed me not, to sanctify me in the eyes of the children of Israel, therefore ye shall not bring this congregation into the land which I have given them.</u>

LESSONS

Dear reader, different spirit of Pisgah(s) exists, namely;
- Pisgah of wealth,
- Pisgah of Marriage;
- Pisgah of Health,
- Pisgah of career etc.

BUT, THE MOST TERRIBLE is the PISGAH OF HEAVEN.
This is a Spirit that seeks to ROB a man or woman from seeing HEAVEN

ONLY JESUS CHRIST CAN ARREST THAT SPIRIT, BUT IN COOPERATION WITH YOU

GOOD NEWS: No matter how great your SINS are, YOU can register for Heaven TODAY, right NOW, and right HERE. Isaiah 1:18, 19. How?
- Simply believe in your heart that Jesus Christ died and Resurrected for YOU, personally. Rom 10 : 9 -10
- Open your mouth and pray, audibly, a prayer of surrender to God, personally, accepting his Gift for you. Rom 10: 9 – 10 , 13

- **DECISION FOR HEAVEN**

<u>IF YOU WANT TO BE WASHED BY THE BLOOD OF JESUS CHRIST</u> , BE BORN AGAIN, AND <u>ESCAPE FROM DEATH TO LIFE (</u> John 5 : 24 <u>),</u> THEN OPEN YOUR MOUTH AND PRAY THE FOLLOWING PRAYERS .

- Lord Jesus Christ, I ACCEPT that I am a sinner. Rom 3:23, Is 64:6, , Ps 51:5
- I REPENT, confess , renounce and for sake my SINS, and receive your forgiveness 1 John 1 : 9
- Wash my Sins away with your precious blood, shed on Calvary Cross

for me. Heb 9:22, 12
- Lord Jesus Christ, come into my heart today and be my Lord and Savior. I dedicate the rest of my life to you Rev 3 : 20, Joshua 24 : 15b
- Thank you Jesus that I am now born again, and for saving me. John 3: 3

a **DECLARATION OF WAR AGAINST;** The Spirit of PISGAH
Dear reader, remember, the Bible says;
"Death and life are in the power of the tongue: and they that love it shall eat the fruit thereof" Proverbs 18:21

Remember, the Jesus said;
"For by thy words thou shalt be justified, and by thy words thou shalt be condemned" Matthew 12:37

Remember, the Jesus said;
"And from the days of John the Baptist until now the kingdom of heaven suffereth violence, and the violent take it by force." Matthew 11:12

In effect, the power to make changes in your entire destiny is in your tongue, and this includes your salvation. If you choose to keep quiet, you lose the power to influence the happenings in your life. What you say is heard by both God and Satan. And although what you say may seem to you like mere words, they are actually not; for they set things in motion in the realm of the spirit or supernatural.

Remember Jesus said;
"….. the words that I speak unto you, they are spirit, and they are life. " John 6:63. You are also made in God's image, and what you also say "….they are spirit, and they are life." John 6:63

In effect, God expects you to be truly Born Again, and as His child, authoritatively, now act like Jesus Christ did, in the use of your tongue to influence your own destiny and those of others you interact with.

Found below are several prayer topics. Please, open your mouth; and use your mouth and tongue to deal aggressively with this first wicked Spirit, which is called the Spirit of PISGAH

Prayer section – Repeatedly, pray audibly and aggressively
1. Father, I surrender my entire LIFE to you, take over every secret battle in my life, in the name of Jesus Christ, amen
2. By the blood of Jesus Christ of Nazareth, I paralyze any Spirit of Pisgah that seeks to deprive me of Rapture, in the name of Jesus Christ, Amen
3. By the power of the Holy Ghost, I bind any spirit of 'last- minute-error', operating secretly in my life, in the name of Jesus Christ, Amen
4. Any wicked power, seeking to pitch me against the Great and the Terrible God, and to deprive me of making Heaven, be arrested, bound and sent to the abyss, in the name of Jesus Christ, Amen
5. By the power of the almighty God, I curse any spirit of Pisgah, which is operating secretly in any department of my life, in then name of Jesus Christ, Amen
6. Any invisible Anti-Rapture rope, tied to my life, catch fire, break and release me forever, for God's kingdom, in the name of Jesus Christ, Amen
7. Any silent Spirit of Pisgah, hiding in my life, hoping to strike on the day of Rapture, be consumed by the consuming fire of the Great God Jehovah, in the name of Jesus Christ, Amen

CONFESSIONS
Please, confess the following powerfully again and again.

Confession 1
"Our soul is escaped as a bird out of the snare of the fowlers: the snare is broken, and we are escaped. 124:8 Our help is in the name of the LORD, who made heaven and earth." Psalm 124:7

Confession 2
"No weapon that is formed against thee shall prosper; and every tongue that shall rise against thee in judgment thou shalt condemn. This is the heritage of the servants of the LORD, and their righteousness is of me, saith the LORD." Isaiah 54:17

B The Spirit of SLUMBER and LUKEWARMNESS
This is a spirit that puts a believer to a spiritual sleep, or a state of slumber. Once a person is attacked by this spirit, his or spiritual temperature goes

down. Prayer goes down, Bible studies goes down, and Evangelism goes down etc. The person becomes passive about things of God, and carnality sets in.

The person then becomes insensitive to the things of God, and the voice of God. The root cause for this is the absence of God's fire in the individual. There is no way The Spirit of slumber and lukewarm ness will be comfortable in a person if the one is baptized with the Holy Ghost and with fire. This is one of the many reasons why Jesus instructed his disciplines to tarry in Jerusalem, and to wait for the promise of the Father.

Remember, the Jesus said;
"And, being assembled together with them, commanded them that they should not depart from Jerusalem, but wait for the promise of the Father, which, saith he, ye have heard of me. ..... 1:8 But ye shall receive power, after that the Holy Ghost is come upon you: and ye shall be witnesses unto me both in Jerusalem, and in all Judaea, and in Samaria, and unto the uttermost part of the earth." Acts 1:4-8

Remember, John the Baptist said;
"...., I indeed baptize you with water; but one mightier than I cometh, the latchet of whose shoes I am not worthy to unloose: he shall baptize you with the Holy Ghost and with FIRE." Luke 3:16

Remember, the Jesus said;
"I know thy works, that thou art neither cold nor HOT: I would thou wert cold or hot. 3:16 So then because thou art lukewarm, and neither cold nor hot, I will spue thee out of my mouth." Rev 3:15

The Spirit of slumber and lukewarm ness is a very wicked spirit, capable of robbing a person of being a Rapture-able material, hence the need to declare war on any internal Spirit of slumber and lukewarm-ness, and external arrows of slumber and lukewarm-ness
a **DECLARATION OF WAR AGAINST;** The Spirit of SLUMBER and LUKEWARMNESS

Please, open your mouth; use your mouth and tongue to deal aggressively with this wicked Spirit called The Spirit of slumber and lukewarm-ness

Remember, God's word says;
"Thou shalt also decree a thing, and it shall be established unto thee: and the light shall shine upon thy ways. 22:29 When men are cast down, then thou shalt say, There is lifting up; and he shall save the humble person" Job 22:28

Prayer section – Repeatedly, pray audibly and aggressively
1. Every satanic umbilical cord in my life, still attached to Satan, I cut you off, by sword of fire, in the name of Jesus Christ, Amen.
2. Every Satanic arrow of slumber, fired against my spiritual life, catch fire, burn to ashes in, the name of Jesus Christ, Amen.
3. I drink the blood of Jesus, and eat the coal of fire, therefore my Spirit man catch fire for Jesus, in the name of Jesus Christ, Amen.
4. Holy Ghost fire, purge me from every pollutions of darkness, which are holding me down, and lift me up for Jesus, in the name of Jesus Christ, Amen.
5. Thou Baptizer with the Holy Ghost and with fire, I am ready, visit me now and always, in the name of Jesus Christ, Amen.
6. Father, fill me with power from on high, the power that never could be quenched by the host of darkness, in the name of Jesus Christ, Amen.
7. Lord, use me mightily for the advancement of your kingdom, in the name of Jesus Christ, Amen.

CONFESSIONS
Please, confess the following scriptures, powerfully, again and again.

Confession 1
"… But his word was in mine heart as a burning fire shut up in my bones, and I was weary with forbearing, and I could not stay." Jeremiah 20:9

Confession 2
"Unto thee, O LORD, do I lift up my soul." Psalm 25:1
C   The Spirit of GARMENT DEFILEMENT

The arrow of Garment defilement is the most dangerous 'Anti-Rapture' arrow. What does this mean? This means, once a person's garment is defiled, at the time of the Rapture, the one automatically qualifies as 'left-behind-candidate'.

Hence, Jesus said;
Behold, I come as a thief. Blessed [is] he that watcheth, and <u>keepeth his garments</u>, lest he walk naked, and they see his shame." Revelation 16:15

What is Garment defilement?

When a person becomes Born Again, he or she is given a garment of righteousness, that is, the garment of Jesus Christ replaces the original filthy garment of SIN and death. This garment is needed on the wedding day, when the Bride of Jesus Christ is officially united to Christ, after the Rapture of the Saints. Satan's top-most strategy is to deprive you of being married to Christ, and slide into the category of Tribulation Saints, or Beheaded Saints or even, ultimately, as a Lost Soul in Hell fire.

Hence, spirit of Garment defilement, is the spirit that engineers the pollution of a believer's garment of righteousness. This is due to SIN. Therefore the above warning is not for unbelievers, but rather for a believer, that is born again believer who is expecting to be in Heaven someday. The above scripture is a direct warning regarding the state of a believer's state of righteousness, at the time of Rapture, more than any other time in Christian's life.

The list of SINS that could defile a believer is endless. Hence, the only Antidote is constant cleansing, with the blood of the Lamb of God, through genuine repentance, backed by conscious and deliberate effort to live holy, and ensuring to stay in the Lord's presence, continually.

Living a Holy life depends a lot on the power from within your Spirit man. In effect, the power for holiness comes by tapping from the realm of the supernatural, from the Holy Ghost alone, through constant, and unceasing, prayer, fasting, etc.
It is one of the main reasons Jesus, specifically, said;
"…, that men ought always to pray, and not to faint;" Luke 18:1

Again Jesus, specifically, said regarding Rapture;
Also, He said; "Watch ye therefore, and <u>pray always</u>, that ye may be <u>accounted worthy to escape all these things</u> that shall come to pass, and to stand before the Son of man." Luke 21:36

a DECLARATION OF WAR AGAINST; The Spirit of GARMENT DEFILEMENT

Prayer section

Please, open your mouth; and with your mouth and tongue, decree aggressively against this wicked Spirit, called the Spirit of GARMENT DEFILEMENT.

1. Every root of SIN in my life, I command you uprooted by the fire of God, in the mighty name of Jesus Christ, in the name of Jesus, Amen!
2. Every Anti-Rapture Director of wicked, firing arrow of garment defilement, into my life, be bound, die, in the name of Jesus, Amen!
3. Every satanic iron prison of garment defilement, keeping me in captivity of death, I command you to explode and release me, in the name of Jesus. Amen!
4. Blood of Jesus Christ of Nazareth, break every shackle of SIN in my life, loose me, and redeem me from any wicked Anti-Rapture Spirits, in the name of Jesus. Amen!
5. Every garment-defiling spirit in my life, I command you bound and cast out, in the mighty name of Jesus Christ of Nazareth. Amen!
6. Holy Ghost, envelope me with your fire, and make me Rapture-ready, in the name of Jesus. Amen!
7. God the Holy Ghost charge my Spirit and cloth me your Rapture-readiness garment, in the mighty name of Jesus. Amen!

CONFESSIONS

Please, confess the following powerfully, again and again.

Confession 1: "And the Lord shall deliver me from every evil work, and will preserve me unto his heavenly kingdom: to whom be glory for ever and ever. Amen." 2 Tim 4:18

Confession 2: "He restoreth my soul: he leadeth me in the paths of righteousness for his name's sake." Psalm 23:3

Confession 3: "But thou, O LORD, art a shield for me; my glory, and the lifter up of mine head." Psalm 3:3

Confession 4: "…For thou wilt not leave my soul in hell; neither wilt thou suffer thine Holy One to see corruption…" Psalm 16:10

ABOUT THE AUTHOR

K.N. Arku-Lawson is an Evangelist and a Revivalist. He is the founder of The Price of A Soul Global Outreach Ministry (PASGOM) and also The Escape Route Ministries International (ERMI).

Whilst PASGOM is a purely evangelistic Ministry, (ERMI) worldwide,   is a Revival Ministry, worldwide.

More about the activities of PASGOM may be located at www.pasgom.org, OR www.pasgom.com

K.N. Arku-Lawson is an Engineer, with Bsc from KNUST, Ghana, and also Postgraduate studies in ITC, Netherlands.

K.N. Arku-Lawson is mainly an itinerary Evangelists and a Revivalist. With his powerful presence on the internet, his Evangelistic Ministry cuts across the Globe.

In the area of Revival, he operates with special emphasis on
• Spiritual warfare;
• Strategic Evangelism
• Rapture-Readiness, and the End-Time Events

INVITATION: FOR REVIVAL
If you want to invite Evangelist K. N. Arku-Lawson to your Church for a Revival, email may be sent to;
I.   Revival@pasgom.org   OR   pasgom@gmail.com
ii.   Evangelism@pasgom.org OR   pasgom@gmail.com

GENEAL COMMENTS, CONTACT ETC
Please, after reading this book, if you have comments, remark, criticisms, opinion, or anything statement related to this book, send to any of the following;
FOR GENEAL COMMENTS, REMARKS, OPINION ETC
Please send to any of the following Email addresses;
RaptureMidnight@pasgom.org
RaptureMidnight@gmail.com
RaptureMidnight@yahoo.com

OTHER CONTACTS of Evangelist K.N. Arku-Lawson:;
Telephone: + 233 – (0) 540 – 034 - 958
Email: pasgom@gmail.com
Stay blessed
Evangelist K.N. Arku-Lawson

BEFORE YOU CLOSE THIS BOOK
VERY IMPORTANT:

Considering the seriousness, and also how URGENT, the issues you are about to read in this book are, if you are not yet BORN AGAIN, please, be wise, and seize this opportunity to have your name in the BOOK OF LIFE, without delay, before you finish reading this book. If you wish to do so, follow the steps blow.

STEPS to salvation:
1. Simply believe in your heart that Jesus Christ died for your SINS and Resurrected for YOU, personally. Rom 10 : 9 -10
2. Open your mouth and pray, audibly, a prayer of surrender to God, personally, accepting his Gift for you. Rom 10:9 ,10 , 13

- **DECISION FOR HEAVEN**

IF YOU WANT TO BE WASHED BY THE BLOOD OF JESUS CHRIST, BE BORN AGAIN, AND ESCAPE FROM DEATH TO LIFE (John 5 : 24), THEN OPEN YOUR MOUTH AND PRAY THE FOLLOWING PRAYERS .

PRAYER SECTION
- Lord Jesus Christ, I ACCEPT that I am a sinner. Rom 3:23, Is 64:6, , Ps 51:5
- I REPENT, confess , renounce and forsake my SINS, and receive your forgiveness 1 John 1 : 9
- Wash my Sins away with your precious blood, which was shed on Calvary cross for me. Heb 9:22, 12
- Lord Jesus Christ, come into my heart today and be my Lord and Savior. Rev 3 : 20,
- I dedicate the rest of my life to you. Joshua 24 : 15b
- Thank you Jesus that I am now <u>born again</u>; and for saving me. John 3: 3

IMPORTANT: Always remain faithful to Jesus Christ, loving God with all your heart, and also love your neighbor as yourself.

For you to remain in God's LOVE and grow spiritually;
*   Read the Bible, especially the New Testament, focusing on the Gospel of Matthew, Mark, Luke, and John to know more about Jesus Christ and make Him your friend. 1 Peter 2: 2.
*   Pray always to God Luke 18 : 1
*   Locate a Bible believing church where you can grow. Acts 2:47b
*   Tell others about Christ, continually. Ezekiel 33 : 8

ARE YOU ALREADY BORN AGAIN?
DO YOU DESIRE CLOSER WALK WITH GOD?

*   PRAY AUDIBLY, THE PRAYERS BELOW, IF YOU DESIRE A FAITHFUL AND CLOSER WALK WITH GOD
*   Lord Jesus Christ, from today, my life is open and available for your fresh fire.
*   Lord break me, melt me, mold me, purge me and fill me anew with your Holy oil, and use me greatly for your glory.
*   Lord Jesus, Baptize me with the Holy Ghost and with fire as promised in Luke 3:16;
*   "John answered, saying unto them all, I indeed baptize you with water; but one mightier than I cometh, the latchet of whose shoes I am not worthy to unloose: he shall baptize you with the Holy Ghost and with fire:"
*   Father, let ALL your plans for my life manifest speedily, in accordance with Jeremiah 29:11;
*   "For I know the thoughts that I think toward you, saith the LORD, thoughts of peace, and not of evil, to give you an expected end."
*   Father open my spiritual eyes to see, spiritual ears to hear, and my heart to understand the URGENCY of the issues I am about to read in this book, that is, The End Times events..
*   Lord, empower me; use me; Oh Lord, to gallop, carrying the truth of your word to others, to rescue as many as need to be delivered from darkness to light.

- Lord Jesus , purge me and make me a vessel, ready for the master's use, in accordance with 2 Tim 2:21;
- "If a man therefore purge himself from these, he shall be a vessel unto honor, sanctified, and meet for the master's use, and prepared unto every good work"
- Father, give me Kingdom knowledge and zeal, to understand the times I live in, after the order of the Children of Issachar.
  I Chronicles 12:32

Thank you Father for answered prayers, in the precious name of your Son, Jesus Christ. Amen!

IMPORTANT APPEAL

PLEASE, HELP SPREAD THE INFORMATION ABOUT THE END-TIME EVENTS.

The ultimate GOAL of writing this book is to sensitize as many people as possible across the Globe, concerning this SOON COMING END-TIME EVENTS. And this ought to t be done, as fast as possible, to fight pervasive ignorance in the body of Christ, today, especially about VITAL End –Time issues.

As a key strategy to achieve this, a passionate appeal is being made to CHRISTIANS, worldwide, who lay hands on this BOOK, to assist in disseminating the contents of this book to as many people as possible, both believers and un-believers, worldwide.

If you a Christian reading this book, the appeal to you is this: That you will TARGET AT LEAST TEN (10) PEOPLE, WHO SHOULD HAVE ACCESS TO THE INFORMATION IN THIS BOOK.
This is very IMPORTANT.

With the current modern Technology, no matter where your friends and love ones live on planet Earth, distance cannot be an excuse for not being able to share this VITAL information with them.

Recommended STEPS

- Compile the names and contact of at least TEN (10) people, to whom you wish to pass information about this BOOK.
- Simply inform them to get a copy of this important BOOK.
- If they are far away, send them a message, asking them to visit this page WWW.PASGOM.ORG/BOOK, for extra information.
- You may communicate by Email, Text message, Phone call, etc
- Pray not only for yourself, but also for the Salvation of others. If they are saved, get them Rapture-Ready.. DO NOT DELAY!

Remember Hosea 4:6;
"My people are destroyed for lack of knowledge: because thou hast rejected knowledge…" Hosea 4:6

May God bless you for your OBEDIENCE, as you read and share the content of this BOOK with others!

Evangelist K. N. Arku-Lawson / www.pasgom.org/

Jesus Christ said

"He that is unjust, let him be unjust still: and he which is filthy, let him be filthy still: and he that is righteous, let him be righteous still: and he that is holy, let him be holy still." Revelation 22:11

Jesus said in Mark 4:9

And he said unto them, He that hath ears to hear, let him hear" Mark 4:9

For update of other books by the author of this book, visit *www.pasgom.org/book*

PERSONAL EVANGELISM / BOOK RECOMMENDATION TO OTHERS

Having clearly understood how important I am as a Christian, as a very important channel God wants to use to reach others for Christ; and having clearly understood the URGENCY of the message of this book; the crucial call to Evangelism in general, I personally wish to make the following pledge to God;

- I will obey His command; to GO INTO ALL THE WORLD, AND PREACH THE GOSPEL TO EVERY CREATURE;
- I will constantly pray for all love ones or lost souls listed below
- I will recommend this book to them, to enhance of awareness of others, especially regarding crucial issues of this End-time

Name:... Signature:.......................... Date:........................

No.	Name of your Love Ones	Email	Tel.	Remark
1				
2				
3				
4				
5				

Page No.	YOUR GENERAL COMMENTS / REMARK / OBSERVATIONS ETC

INFORMATION ABOUT THE 4 VERSIONS OF THIS BOOK

Due to the VITAL nature of this End-time message, this book exists in 4 different versions, depending on the number of pages and, therefore, the depth of details captured in it. This is to create flexibility for all types of potential readers; in terms of the time required for reading the entire book, the depth of the knowledge and insight one is looking for, the portability and your affordability of the book, etc. The version of the book you are currently reading is indicated on the bottom-right corner of the front cover.

The versions of this book are;

1. **Expanded Version**   – More than 300 pages
2. **Normal Version**   – Between 200 -300 pages
3. **Abridged Version**   -- Between 100 -200 pages
4. **Compressed version**   -- Between 50 -100 pages